Conte

To Hilary Anne

Foreword

Few tasks can be more searching or self-revealing for a journalist than to pen a personal pilgrimage of reflection. No longer is the task the analysis of a figure already judged by the public, nor an analysis of that person's worth, successes or failures. Nor is it a carefully composed article about some event of public importance.

Instead the journalist must disregard the protection of the critical observer, and depend on a willingness to find honesty in indulging on a journey of self-discovery. That degree of honesty will determine the true nature of what a lifetime of observation of others will tell the writer, and how the gifts of memory and experience have fashioned his own life.

Precious beyond the written words is the self-reflective honesty. Only sometimes can this reflective journey truly achieve self-discovery. If one adds to this the ingredient of faith, then the self-search becomes a journey of inner scrutiny, and also a pilgrimage of heart-searching. In such a situation the reader must ask the question, 'How honest is the writer?'

What follows in this book is just such a journey of self-discovery by one of the most respected journalists in Ireland, whose career has ventured far from the discipline of a writer on religious matters. Alf McCreary is an award-winning journalist whose journey of faith has been a lifetime of recording events, occurrences and human experiences that have fashioned the lives of others. That journey has taken him far beyond the boundaries of his native Northern Ireland and those whose lives are involved with religious matters.

Most people in Northern Ireland will associate the name of Alf McCreary with his commentaries on Churches and religious denominations, but the following pages disclose a panorama of human experience of life which is relevant for people of faith and of non-faith alike. This varies from the author's experience of the sanctuary and the pulpit to the human suffering and disasters that he has witnessed during the years of turmoil in his native province, and much further afield in the developing world. This variety of backgrounds has demanded a personal degree of honesty and truth which I am sure the reader will find on each page.

It has been for me a great privilege to regard the author as a close friend for many years. His writings have involved comments on my own journey of faith from which I have learned – both when he was critical and when he indicated approval. Now he has granted me the privilege of writing this introduction to his journey.

Back in 2022, in a fourth book of poetry and prose produced by a writers' circle that was established some twenty-five years ago by the author, he asked the question of himself, 'Over the years what has happened to Alf McCreary, the human being behind the headlines?' His reflection, among others of that tightly knit group, is different from the Alf McCreary we had become used to. He has revealed a kind of freedom of expression that we did not always find in his commentary on church matters. I detect that welcome freedom in what he writes in the following pages, which might inspire and challenge us to ask the same question he asked himself in 2022.

A personal expression of faith is above all a deeply private matter. On occasions we encounter someone who wishes to share with us its importance in their life. Equally, a person's lifestyle or attitude to events will tell us a great deal about their own values and beliefs, but on the whole, nearly all questions about faith remain private. For Alf McCreary this book encroaches on the private side, mainly through that other human element which we can best describe as experience. What he has seen, heard and encountered as a person and as a professional commentator has shaped and fastened what he now learns about himself.

From his early days in the village of Bessbrook in South Armagh, where we are introduced to family values with a certain feeling of early emotional loss, and his gradual recognition of the importance of a relatively settled background, and on to his adult years with their human and professional awareness of a land in bitter conflict and of great suffering and distress, Mr McCreary shares with us his mindset and outlook, which ask so many questions. In fact there are pages where he asks questions of deeper significance than even he may recognise. He describes events and personalities, and leaves us to draw our own conclusions.

Is this Alf McCreary the professional at work? His compassion appears most clearly when he reacts to the experience of individuals faced with the trauma of life or death. Not for the first time he describes his encounters and relationships with that saintly pair Senator Gordon Wilson and his wife Joan from Enniskillen. No one could fail to be moved by their experience of the death of their beloved daughter Marie, who was one of the victims of the no-warning Provisional IRA bomb that exploded at the local cenotaph where people had gathered on Remembrance Sunday in 1987.

His words vividly capture that deeply moving human tragedy. The spontaneous reaction of Gordon Wilson in bearing no 'ill-will' during a BBC Radio interview on the evening of the bomb stunned the world, and Alf McCreary takes us to the heart of that Christian witness. His words have the ring of truth, as I recall my own memories of kneeling beside Gordon Wilson in the Enniskillen hospital on that fateful day, but perhaps we can read a great deal about the writer himself as he reacts to it all. His words go far beyond the striking description of this heart-breaking event, to a human recognition of the ultimate triumph of a truly Christian witness. For Alf McCreary the observer there is a communion of understanding that goes beyond detailed description. There is a kindred recognition of a belief in a Christian faith that mattered.

This same sympathy which moves beyond comprehensive descriptive writing appears again and again when he turns to many other events during the landmarks of the Northern Ireland Troubles, such as the Kingsmills massacre when, in January 1976, eleven innocent Protestant workmen were gunned down by Republican paramilitaries in cold blood on a dark and lonely country road in South Armagh, not so far from Mr McCreary's native village. The only survivor, Alan Black, was well known to the author as a fellow villager. The same professional detachment overlying his acute compassion for people is also clear in his reports from postwar Vietnam and Cambodia as well as the more recent upheavals in Rwanda, Sri Lanka and elsewhere.

These writings are such a contrast to his reporting on purely church trends and events. In former days, when the Irish media carried many more stories about major meetings ,including Church of Ireland general synods, Presbyterian general assemblies and Methodist conferences, or other important ecclesiastical developments, there was an anticipation as to how the newspaper and broadcast journalists would report these gatherings.

Today the declining media interest in such matters, in response to dwindling reader interest, has changed the demands on Alf McCreary's time and energies. Gone are the headlines that church people used to anticipate eagerly, and a media that has reflected the changing importance of religion has moved on, as has the significance of the religion correspondents.

Perhaps it is this change itself which has contributed to Alf McCreary's timing in writing this book. His reflections are of a memory that is rich in value. Yet in his honesty of experience there is a nostalgia that itself adds a relevance to his reactions to human emotions. In discovering what these memories have contributed to his self-searching, there are truths which are just as relevant today as they ever were.

This book is a most readable account of the life of a compassionate observer of human nature. The depth of this account owes much to Mr McCreary's interest in people, and perhaps without him realising it, that interest has contributed greatly to his personal faith. The reader can draw his or her own conclusions about the effects that various events and people have had on the author's personal thinking. Dare I suggest also that his friends will detect once more the significant faith influence of his wife Hilary?

What we have here is a writer who is prepared to observe life, people and situations with a remarkable degree of human understanding. He has moved beyond any denominational interpretation of belief and has found in his observance of others a faith that endures far beyond the walls of a single religious label. This discovery gives a further dimension to Alf McCreary's writings, which in themselves bear witness to a continuing and deeply questioning journey of faith.

The Right Reverend The Lord Eames OM

Introduction

The continuing situation in Northern Ireland has been one of those seemingly endless deadlocks that few outsiders, particularly English politicians, can begin to understand. Even people like me, who have lived, worked and raised families through the worst of the Troubles here are uncertain about what the future will hold for all of us in Ireland, or indeed for all the people in these islands.

However, everyone agrees that at the heart of the long conflict between Orange and Green over many years is the baleful intermingling of religion and politics. As a long-time senior journalist with the *Belfast Telegraph*, and as a freelance writer for many other publications at home and abroad, I have covered almost every dimension of this tortuous story.

I have written much elsewhere about my own life and career, and now, to mark my sixtieth anniversary as a professional writer, I have a compulsion – call it what you will – to look back reflectively and philosophically on some of the people who have impressed me most for good or ill, and also on the best and worst of religious practice in Ireland, which used to be called 'the Island of Saints and Scholars'.

Religion has earned a deservedly bad press in recent years, but I worry that in our increasingly secular society we are rejecting far too easily some of the visions and best standards of the Christian faith, which has provided the bedrock of our civilisation for over 2,000 years.

I think it is timely to remind people that a deep religious faith can dramatically change lives for the better, and that it can also sustain individuals and families in times of great suffering and distress. It is equally important to remind ourselves that the misuse and debasement of religion can itself cause immense pain.

I hope that in retelling part of my own story, with fresh insights gained from a long experience of living and working through the upheavals here and elsewhere, I can help other people to understand more about the pressures and realities of a divided society, through the eyes of a young boy who became a journalist and reported on decades of one of the most frightening conflicts in recent Anglo-Irish history. The experiences gained in my own land have also helped me to understand better the trauma within the conflicts of other divided societies.

In this book I will also reflect upon the influences in my early and later life that helped me to shape my own path as I reported on so many disturbing events during the Troubles at home, and also overseas, including in countries of the developing world in Africa, Asia and Latin-America. Paradoxically I also found reassurance and inspiration in many of these places during the worst of times.

I do not offer any solutions to the 'Northern Ireland' problem or the problems of any divided society, but I pay tribute to those people who have helped and inspired me, and to those whose faith-based lives have been reassuring and inspiring to many others.

In writing this book, I am conscious of starting out on an adventure of my own. I do not know where it will take me, or what it will reveal about myself or my experiences of living in a complex and fascinating society, despite its violence and deadlock. However, I hope that you will stay with me as I follow that journey to wherever it leads us.

Alf McCreary,
Belfast,
17 March 2024

1

First Steps

I first heard about someone or something called 'God' when I was five, just at the end of the Second World War. This introduction to the Great Unknown took place during my first experience of Sunday school in the Presbyterian church at Bessbrook, which was situated in South Armagh near the border with the Republic of Ireland.

My Sunday school teacher, Anson Chapman, was a kindly man who worked as an insurance agent in the model village of Bessbrook. He was teaching a small group of us, in a balcony corner of the nineteenth-century church, about the words of a children's hymn written by the nineteenth-century itinerant American hymn-writer Philip Bliss. It assured me that 'God is always near me, / Hearing What I Say, / Knowing All My Thoughts and Deeds, / All my Work and Play'.

That seemed fair enough to me, but there was more. God was also near me 'In the Darkest Night, / He can see me just the same, as by midday light'. Then there was more reassurance in the last verse. I was told that God was always near me, 'Though so young and small, / Not a look or word or thought, / But God knows it all'.

That was a lot for a five-year-old to take in, but it did not worry me unduly. With a childish faith I accepted this as part of the normal order of things. God was in his heaven and all was well with the world. It seemed as natural as the sparkling water in the pond that drove the machinery in the local linen mill, or the flowers and leaves of the hedgerows in the beautiful village of Bessbrook.

There was one worry, however. When I misbehaved at home, as small boys do, I was told that God had a big black book, and if I did anything wrong or was naughty he would put a tick against my name. That was a very serious black mark. In other words, I could not just do as I liked, and if I disobeyed the rules, there would be a day of reckoning. So I began to think that this God was not just a bearded old man sitting magically on a cloud and holding a harp, but that he was keeping a beady eye on me as well. In some ways that childish awe of an ultimate judgement never really left me.

For the most part, however, I had a happy early childhood untroubled by religion. I continued to attend Sunday school and church every week, not out of conviction but because I had no choice. In those days everyone was made to go to church, and Sunday school was quite pleasant – partly because I met most of my nursery and primary school friends there. In those days the church was also known as the 'Meeting House', because it was where people from the village and the surrounding farms could meet regularly.

The services could seem long and a bit boring at times, but when that happened I used to try to count the particles of dust caught in the sunbeams shining through the church window. However, there were also big rewards for such long-term patience .

For example there was the annual excursion from the village to the heady delights of the seaside town of Warrenpoint, which was always such an attractive place for me, despite its heavily cobbled beach. The excursion began at around 8 o'clock on a Saturday morning, with a parade down from the church and through the village, accompanied by our local flute band and a large group of parents and friends ready to enjoy a day out.

There was also the unspeakable delight of travelling in a clanking and sooty steam train from Newry to Warrenpoint, and then to enjoy a picnic of sandwiches and fizzy drinks which, like ice-cream, was a rarity in those days just at the end of the rationing of the Second World War. All of these delights were due to my membership of the Sunday school – a little bit of learning from the Scriptures each week seemed a good deal in return for such treats.

For years I went regularly to Sunday school and church services, and I learned by heart all the important Bible texts, which unfortunately I forgot almost entirely later on. Each year there was an examination when we were quizzed individually by Sunday school teachers from other Presbyterian churches in rural South Armagh. I was always nervous but the inquisitors were usually friendly men (always men) with the large hands of farmers and agricultural folk, and a reassuring manner. I always passed with a 100 per cent record, except for one terrible year when I misquoted or forgot the comment by the centurion at Christ's crucifixion: 'Truly this was the Son of God.' I was bitterly disappointed by my failure, but the hurt soon wore off.

When I hear or read that passage of Scripture I am reminded of my perceived failure so long ago, and I always smile at my memory of the 1965 biblical film epic *The Greatest Story Ever Told*, when John Wayne played the Roman centurion and uttered the immortal words, 'Truly this was the Son of Gawd.' Clearly by divine magic, the centurion had morphed from being a Roman at the time of Jesus Christ's death, to an American in the Hollywood heyday of the twentieth century. The story is told, true or not, that the film director George Stevens advised Wayne to deliver his lines with a sense of awe, so he duly obliged in the next take by saying, 'Aww, truly this was the Son of Gawd.'

Bessbrook was not short of churches. On the winding road leading down from the convent of the Sisters of Mercy situated on a big hill overlooking the village there were several religious buildings. On the left was my own Presbyterian church, with a gorgeous view over the valley and the Craigmore Viaduct, which carried the Belfast to Dublin steam train on its daily journeys to and from the two capitals of a divided island. In my boyhood

I sometimes walked across that viaduct with my school friends, even though it was strictly illegal to do so.

Later I discovered that it had been built by the celebrated nineteenth-century Irish railway engineer William Dargan from County Laois, who also helped to excavate many thousands of tons of silt from Belfast Lough to make way for the establishment of shipbuilding in the city. This is where the firm of Harland and Wolff established their world-class shipyard, which produced many hundreds of vessels of all kinds, including the infamous *Titanic*, which collided with an iceberg in the North Atlantic in 1912 and sank with the loss of over 1,500 lives.

Over seventy years earlier Dargan was making the first of the 'cuts' through the deep mudbanks in Belfast Lough to help larger vessels moor nearer the centre of the city. The excavated mud, known as the 'spoil', was used to form an island near the larger quays, and became known as Dargan's Island. Later the name was changed by the Belfast Harbour Commissioners to Victoria Island in honour of the young Queen, who came to Belfast during her visit to Ireland in 1849.

I was unaware of all this complicated Irish history during my early boyhood, or the significance of being a 'Protestant' through an accident of birth, but many years later being perceived as a Protestant from South Armagh gave me an automatic identity of being an Ulster Unionist, whether I actually was or not.

Near my own church in Bessbrook was the Anglican church, a tall building with a big spire, and architecturally totally different from the somewhat squat Presbyterian church. I used to go to this Anglican church roughly once a year, for the Boy Scouts and Wolf Cub services, to which we marched in our uniforms. This was to mark St George's Day in honour of the adopted English saint, but I cannot remember any service in Bessbrook to honour our own patron, St Patrick. It just didn't seem to matter in those days, though – for some reason I could not fathom – I was drawn much later to Patrick, and wrote several books about him. I found the Anglican liturgy in Bessbrook much more interesting than the Presbyterian services, partly because we had to stand up quite a lot. This prevented us from falling asleep during the sermon. I was also fascinated by the robed male clergy, who looked almost as if they were wearing frocks!

Further down the road was the Roman Catholic chapel, but I never entered the building because I had no reason to do so. Ecumenical services were unheard of, so the inside of the chapel remained a mystery to me. I discovered much more about the denominational divisions in the village later, and I had no bias against Catholics. I once overheard people talking about the years after the Partition of Ireland when a local member of the B-Specials police force had fired a bullet through a window of the chapel as his patrol car was driven past the building. I don't know whether he was drunk or bigoted or both. Some people found that story quite amusing but I thought as a boy that it was sad, and very rude and unfair to the Catholic people in the village.

Still further down the road leading to the centre of Bessbrook was the small Methodist church where people worshipped early on Christmas morning after singing carols as they walked along the streets of the village from 6 o'clock. I once joined them, and found it a magical experience, and a bit like the writer Laurie Lee's beautiful description of similar Christmas celebrations in his native village of Stroud in England. In those Christmas mornings of my boyhood, the Incarnation of the Christ child seemed very real to me, but so too did Santa Claus.

There were other small denominational groupings in the village, including a few Plymouth Brethren, who seemed remote and kept themselves to themselves. I also attended a weekly service for children which was organised by a decent and very born-again Christian man called Johnny Qua. I remember one day that he was in great pain, and he prayed that the Good Lord would heal his back. I was very impressed, and surprised to realise that you could pray to God to help deal with the pain in your back as well as to save your soul. I never found out whether Johnny's back was eventually healed by prayer or not, but certainly he was fit enough to take us on his own 'wee trip' to Rostrevor once a year. We enjoyed our fizzy drinks and sandwiches and a climb up through the forest glades to a clearing called Fiddler's Green and a view of the Big Stone, which had been deposited high on a hill overlooking Carlingford Lough.

This huge granite boulder, weighing some 50 tonnes, was thought to have been transported from Scotland and deposited some 10,000 years earlier during the last Ice Age. Local legend suggested that it had actually been hurled from the Cooley Mountains across Carlingford Lough by the Irish giant Finn McCool, and landed on a flat space on the hillside above Rostrevor. All of this geology and fantasy was too complicated for small boys like us, who were just happy to visit the Big Stone and have lots of fun.

When the 'wee trip' was over we returned, tired but happy, by bus to Bessbrook, where we formed a circle in the village square and somewhat embarrassingly sang the Doxology: 'Praise God from whom all blessings flow, / Praise Him his creatures here below, / Praise Him above ye Heavenly hosts, / Praise Father, Son and Holy Ghost'. Whenever I hear this sung on solemn and very holy church occasions. I always think of Johnny Qua, and his bad back, and our 'wee trip' to Rostrevor.

I was almost surrounded by churches in my childhood, but not suffocated by them. I never felt that religion was being thrust down my throat. It made me realise, however, that there were people from different religious backgrounds, including various Protestant denominations, and also Catholics, although I never seemed to meet any Catholics in my early days. I discovered later on that Bessbrook had been founded in 1845 by the Quaker Richardson family from Warwickshire in England, and that there were still Quakers in our village who worshipped in a small church situated in the woods near the big linen mill. I was well 'churched' in my boyhood, and my faith journey had begun.

Nevertheless, I never became 'saved' or 'born again', but I realised that there were many good people who went to church, and who knew the difference between right and wrong. One of those who impressed me most was the Presbyterian minister Reverend Sidney Carser. He had come to Bessbrook after an early career in engineering in Belfast, and he stayed in the village for the whole of his long ministry.

He was a well-built, stocky man with a broad smile, a kindly face behind his big spectacles, and a warm friendly manner. He was widely revered in the village for his work as a pastor, and as a church leader. When he visited the homes of his flock, on a carefully prepared schedule, they brought out the best crockery, as well as buns, making for calorie-laden occasions, however well meant. Mr Carser kept hens in the field between the Manse and the graveyard, and this somehow gave a down-to-earth dimension to such a saintly man.

He had some difficult times in the village, including the two separate occasions when he had to inform my Granny McCreary's sister, known as 'Aunt' Maria, that two of her sons had died during the Second World War, one of them amid the horrors of a Japanese prisoner-of-war camp. No one could have passed on that tragic news with more sympathy and Christian comfort than Mr Carser.

I thought that he was a remarkable example of someone demonstrating so visibly and naturally the loving Gospel he preached. If Christianity could produce someone like that, I reckoned that there was bound to be much more to it than I had been able to recognise, or was willing to admit.

So, in my earliest days, my Presbyterian church gave me a sense of warmth and of belonging, even if I did not really understand what that meant at the time. I was not to know then that the very same building many years later would be part of the aftermath for me of one of the most tragic and savage multiple murders of my lifetime.

2

The Model Village

Bessbrook village was known by many people as 'the model village' because it had no pawnshops or public houses or police for many decades after its establishment in 1845 by the Quaker Richardson family, who had emigrated from England during the reign of King James I.

However, the nearby village of Camlough had more than its share of pubs, as well as a bar known as The Pit in Millvale, on the other side of the village. All of these hostelries were within walking distance of Bessbrook, so in reality those who could not get a drink in the village did not have far to travel to slake their thirst.

Bessbrook eventually had a police station, and this was particularly important for security during the many violent incidents along the Irish border. However, with the reorganisation of police resources in the North more than 150 years later, the Bessbrook station was closed. Initially, however, the early absence of police, pawnbrokers and pubs in Bessbrook was evidence that the establishment of the village was part of a remarkable social experiment by its founder, John Grubb Richardson, who was putting into practice his strong Quaker principles of social reform, temperance and non-violence.

He was a man of firm views, and in 1882 he refused a baronetcy from Prime Minister William Gladstone for his 'public services'. Richardson replied to Gladstone, 'I belong to the Society of Friends, some of whose members in early days resigned their titles for conscience's sake ... I feel as if the acceptance of your offer on the grounds of having tried to do a little for the benefit of my fellow men would detract from the satisfaction I have found in so doing.'[1]

A textile business had been carried on in Bessbrook by John Pollock and his family since 1761. It was bought by a Joseph Nicholson in 1802, who in turn sold it in 1845 to the Richardsons. They further developed the manufacture of linen to a very high quality for a wide home and export market.

John Grubb Richardson and his family did not try to impose 'Quakerism' as a requirement for employment in their factory, and the villagers went about their business with or without the influence of the other mainstream Christian churches in the village. However, in the local 'Institute', known colloquially as the 'Town Hall', there was a large mural behind the stage where musical performances and other social events frequently took place. It was therefore unavoidably visible to everyone, and the message was clear: 'In Essentials, Unity, in non-Essentials, Liberty, in All Things, Charity'. This quotation has been wrongly attributed to St Augustine as well as to a sixteenth-century Italian bishop and a seventeenth-century Lutheran pastor in Germany. Whatever its origins, it seemed to me to be an admirable philosophy for Bessbrook.

It was a model village in the sense that people had a strong community spirit in the days when labour was hard and money was scarce. That spirit was fostered by social and sporting events, and by strong neighbourly ties when people depended on help from one another, and they had to share in making their own amusements outside working hours.

There was no television until the early 1950s, with an often flickering reception in black and white only, but there were many concerts in the Town Hall, where the villagers displayed an impressive talent for drama, music, dancing and storytelling. These fostered a sense of community without the distraction of our modern times, when we have so many television channels and other forms of communication. Deciding which one to choose can cause a degree of stress.

People have never before had access to such a range of opportunities for communication, but so little incentive to communicate with one another. Today's social media rule supreme, but not necessarily for the better.

Perhaps in looking back from this distance, there is a temptation to remember Bessbrook as more of a model village than it actually was. It had its share of suicides, including those of the local rector and our family doctor, as well as unhappy relationships, and the financial worries of people working in the local mill whose future depended almost solely on the vagaries of the textile trade. Despite all of that, the Bessbrook of my boyhood and youth had a kind of innocence that sadly has been lost for ever in a modern world where people seem to matter less than economic progress and the inevitable assessment of that progress, or otherwise, in monetary terms only.

However, there was another dimension to Bessbrook. There was no obvious friction between Protestants and Catholics, and no sense of threat from either side of the baleful religious divide that was tragically evident in many Catholic or Protestant areas in other places, and notably in the cities of Belfast and Derry/ Londonderry.

Yet, despite the generally good community relations in Bessbrook, there was a subtle difference beneath the surface. At one level, religion did not seem to matter very much, but at another level it mattered a great deal.

There was welcome cooperation in sport. For example, Catholic and Protestant footballers, and perhaps even a couple of agnostics or atheists, were members of the Bessbrook Strollers soccer team which won the Irish Junior Cup in 1945. This was a magnificent achievement for a group from a small rural village, and I recall the great excitement at such a remarkable success, partly because my much-loved Uncle Bill, who was like a big brother to me, was part of that team.

Bessbrook may also have had a mixed rugby team when it won the Irish Towns Cup three times, in 1885, 1887 and 1888, and shared it with Dungannon in 1886. These were also magnificent sporting achievements. Sadly, however, rugby was abandoned in the village after one of the players, their captain, Tom McGaffin, died while playing in the semi-final of the Towns Cup against City of Derry in 1896.

The Nationalist community also had great success in sport, including Gaelic football, with the well-known Bessbrook Geraldines winning the County Armagh Senior Championship in 1909, 1916 and 1939.[2]

People shared in the enjoyment of sporting success, and in other ways. As a child I recall a group of Catholic and Protestant men who formed an unofficial choir around the 'Big Tree' in the centre of the village, just outside my bedroom in Wakefield Terrace. Sadly, the Big Tree and the singers have long gone, but that sense of togetherness lingers on in my mind. So too does the memory of a mixed group of villagers who went for a drink on Saturdays in a hotel in Omeath across the border, and ended the evening by sharing in the singing of the Twenty-third Psalm.

There was also great neighbourliness in Bessbrook. Our next-door neighbours in Wakefield Terrace were Catholics, as were our neighbours in The Gardens housing estate where my grandfather Tommy McCreary and I lived with his daughter Jean and her husband Denzil and their family after my grandmother Mary Anne (Minnie) died. My grandfather had become my guardian after I was born out of wedlock to my teenage mother Lena and my slightly older father Norman, who did not marry her. To be fair to both of them, I heard later on that Norman had offered to marry Lena but my grandmother told him that he was not good enough, partly because he was unemployed. That stung and hurt him so much that he later went to England and did so well in business that he became a multimillionaire. My mother left the McCreary home when I was five years old to marry a man called John Black. They had a long and happy marriage, and had five children.

My grandfather was a member of the Orange Order and his next-door neighbour Oliver McElherron was a drummer in the

'Green' accordion band, which celebrated various Irish Nationalist events in the village each year. Despite the cultural differences, both families were always helpful to each other, and there was never any friction, even on those occasions when Oliver was practising his drums, and the 'boom-boom' filtered through the wall into our small living-room where we watched television.

All our Catholic neighbours on that estate remained great friends with my Aunt Jean, even throughout the Troubles. Some journalists and commentators have painted a picture of a Northern Ireland where Catholics and Protestants were often in bitter conflict with one other, but in my early years in Bessbrook the reality was thankfully different.

Nevertheless, I could never really understand why Protestants and Catholics needed to wear Orange or Green sashes and to parade along different routes in the village at different times to demonstrate their religious and political beliefs. Significantly, however, I was too young to realise that my generation of Catholic as well as Protestant children was being programmed to conform to rules that were not of our making but which were storing up trouble for the future.

There was a prevailing loyalty to the religious denominations in the village, but also to Unionist and Irish Nationalist parties which promised a better future. For more than a century thus far they have failed dismally to make Northern Ireland work as a political entity.

However, there was a dimension in which religion really did matter to God-fearing people in Bessbrook. Occasionally there were Protestant evangelical meetings in the local town hall where the main objective was to save souls and win converts for the Kingdom. I was fascinated by those who bravely rose up from their seats, walked to the front and publicly gave their lives to Christ, though secretly I thought that those who were not 'saved' had a better time. There were too many rules if you were saved, and some of the converts seemed to be missing a bit of joy and laughter. It reminds me of a remark made many years later by the wonderful entertainer and song-writer Leonard Cohen, who told his audiences that he had spent many years searching for wisdom through the teachings of the world's great religions, 'but cheerfulness kept breaking through'.

Mixed marriages between Protestants and Catholics were not encouraged, not only because it appeared to be a big step to take theologically but also because the Catholic Church insisted that the children of the marriage must be brought up as Catholics. That caused much resentment among Protestant families and also great heartache, because in many cases the man or woman who had 'turned' was also turned away by his or her family. This may be incomprehensible in modern times, but to my generation it was religion at its worst.

The perceived difference between Catholics and Protestants was symbolised by the Angelus bells that rang out from the Sisters of Mercy convent, which at one time had some sixty nuns living there. The large building was set on a high hill overlooking the village, but the bells were not intrusive as they wafted over the valley each day. However, when I heard them I sometimes wondered what that convent was really like inside. It was not forbidden for me to go there, but equally there was no reason for me to do so.

Many years later, when I was a university student working in the Bessbrook Post Office to help with the Christmas mail, I had to deliver a telegram to a nun in the convent. In those days a paper telegram was very important, and it could bring good or bad news to the recipient.

So I knocked on the convent door nervously. Eventually footsteps echoed down a corridor, and a young nun opened the door. When she saw the telegram in my hand she became nervous, but once she had read the name on the envelope she said with relief, 'Oh, thank God it's not for me.' This made me realise for the first time that nuns living behind the big walls of a convent were also human beings. Even now it shocks me to admit that I knew so little about how the other half lived.

Despite the drawbacks, I learned a great deal from the local people and from their respect for each other even if they did not go to the same church.

I also learned a great deal from the example of my grandfather Tommy, an Orangeman who reached out to all his neighbours. He once told me that he became an Orangemen because his local Orange hall was the only centre of Protestant social life in rural areas. They held dances and soirées there, and he met young people of his own age. He played Irish jigs on his fiddle, and loved Irish traditional music all his life.

He was born in 1891, and he could trace his father John's birth to 1846, at the time of the Irish Famine, though he never talked about his ancestry. He was a faithful though not strict Presbyterian who went to church every week. He polished his black shoes on a Saturday night but not on the sabbath. However, he was fond of a drink, and sometimes he would travel to Warrenpoint on Sunday afternoon to sit in a large open rowing boat with several others as they made their way across the choppy waters of Carlingford Lough to Omeath in the Irish Republic, where the pubs were open on Sundays, unlike those in Northern Ireland.

Tommy McCreary saw no paradox in going to church on a Sunday morning and then sometimes setting off for a drink in the afternoon. This reminds me of a comment I heard much later from a Presbyterian minister who preached on the Gospel exhortation that you 'cannot serve God and Mammon'. He said, 'In reality many of us manage to do this very nicely.'

My grandfather had been a soldier in the First World War. He joined the Army as '14499 Fus. T. McCreary' in the Royal Irish Fusiliers to take the place of his younger brother Sandy who had fibbed about his birth date and joined up under age. Tommy had been a stretcher-bearer at the Battle of the Somme, but he rarely talked about those horrendous experiences. He once reminisced to my Aunt Jean about carrying a wounded soldier on a stretcher from the front line to a medical outpost for treatment, and having to watch while the surgeons amputated the poor man's leg without an anaesthetic. All they could offer him to deaden the pain was a few mouthfuls of whiskey.

Tommy McCreary had his own painful memories. While he was serving at the Somme in 1916 his mother died, but he never talked about his loss. Nearly sixty years later his elder son Jimmy died from tuberculosis at a young age. My grandfather belonged to a generation of men who were stoic about the hard times in their lives. There was no counselling or psychiatric help available, so they just got on with it.

Back in civilian life Tommy McCreary became a civil servant in the Newry 'Buroo' office where he assisted people claiming unemployment benefit. Sometimes he travelled to Crossmaglen, a staunchly Republican area in South Armagh, where he helped men to sign on for their benefits. Afterwards they would sometimes drink together in a local pub. Tommy was Orange, and they were Green, but over a few pints of Guinness their religious and political labels did not seem to matter.

My grandfather was a kind man, and although he was not 'saved' in the strict Protestant evangelical sense of that term, he had more than enough practical Christianity to adopt me legally when it was suggested in my wider family that I should be adopted, because of the 'shame' that had been brought on all of us. He said, 'There will be no adoption. I will take care of my grandson.' I loved him for that, and for so much else.

For many years I carried the deep emotional scars of being termed 'illegitimate', a stigma that struck at the heart of many an innocent child. In retrospect I am horrified by what happened to many unmarried mothers and their offspring who were treated so cruelly by society and by Catholic and Protestant church authorities in those terrible days. So much for their 'love of God', but not of their fellow human beings, and especially the young unmarried mothers and their children.

I am also aware that I might have been one of the unlucky ones to be handed over by my family to a future unknown, like so many others, but I was so fortunate to be have been embraced in the arms of love by my grandfather, my Aunt Jean and Uncle Denzil and my Uncle Bill, and brought up with respect and hope, and a sense of belonging to my McCreary family.

My grandfather also gave me another important and enduring legacy. By his outlook and actions he showed me that someone could be stereotyped as part of the Orange or Green tribe, but that they could also live a non-tribal life, reaching out to others on all sides. This was certainly true in his time, though attitudes hardened later. His example stayed with me during my career. For many decades I have written extensively for newspapers and in books about some of the most bitter sectarian attitudes and actions imaginable during the Troubles, and in other places far beyond the island of Ireland.

The Orange and Green were labels, but I knew from my upbringing that beyond those labels there was flesh and blood, and that I had to remain aware always that I was writing about suffering and vulnerable human beings on all sides. I owe my grandfather so much for his love and protection when I was young and vulnerable, and above all for showing me how to live a life beyond the Orange and Green or Unionist and Nationalist straitjackets. He died peacefully at the age of eighty-three more than fifty years ago, but I still smile fondly when I think of him. I will treasure his memory until my dying day.

3

Worlds Apart

The children of my generation (from the mid-1940s to the end of the 1950s and beyond) were educated poles apart. The vast majority of Catholic and Protestant girls and boys did not meet each other across the religious divides of a fractured Irish society which was still trying to recover from the trauma of the partition of the island in 1921.

In my native village in South Armagh the Catholic children went to a school near the chapel, or to the convent, while the Protestant children were schooled at the other end of Bessbrook, just opposite the town hall. My primary school, which segregated boys and girls, was Dickensian in its primitive facilities, and its male teachers resorted too easily to bullying and physical punishment.

My school principal was James Darragh, a small tweedy man covered in chalk dust from the blackboard. He had a quick temper, and a frayed billiard cue which he used to mete out punishment much too frequently. 'Jemmy', as he was called, could be described as 'fair', because he punished everybody more or less equally. Those were the days when parents or guardians had no influence on the teachers and the classrooms. I remember an occasion when the mother of a boy came to the school to remonstrate with Jemmy, and he slammed the door in her face.

In his defence, if there is any defence for such behaviour, Mr Darragh must have felt immensely frustrated because almost all his pupils were destined to work in the local linen mill. There

31

were very few educational stars who moved upwards to join the middle-class professions of law, medicine or the Church. It was only later, with the passing of the 1947 Education Act in Northern Ireland, that young people of ability were given the lifeline of attempting to pass an examination called the Eleven-Plus, which opened the door to grammar school and, perhaps, university.

Father Denis Faul, the well-known civil rights activist priest and teacher from Dungannon, later noted perceptively that the 1947 Education Act was a revolutionary piece of legislation because it helped to galvanise a whole generation of Catholic young people who had the benefits of second- and third-level education. This in turn gave them the confidence to spearhead the civil rights movement which, from the late 1960s, radically transformed the political landscape in Northern Ireland.

All of this was a long way from the years I spent in Bessbrook Primary School, where the emphasis was on reading, writing and arithmetic, and little else. Our geography lessons had a distinctly British emphasis because we were obliged to memorise the main textile towns in the North of England, and woe betide anyone who failed to come up with the correct answer. Jemmy Darragh put the fear of God into us, although not necessarily in the biblical sense of 'fearing God'.

I had no sense of 'Irishness' in that school, even though I lived in the North of Ireland. The nearest to anything 'Irish' we encountered was learning to sing Percy French songs, and 'The Minstrel Boy', written by Thomas Moore.

In retrospect, my lack of any Irish identity was extraordinary in a village that was only a few miles from the Irish Republic. Even more extraordinary was the fact that only a mile from my primary school was the historic Derrymore House, where the Act of Union of 1801 was reputedly drawn up by Lord Castlereagh and the Rt Hon Isaac Corry, MP for Newry, who was the Chancellor of the Exchequer in the Irish parliament in Dublin. This attractive thatched house with its granite chimneys is thought to have been built about 1785 and was Corry's summer retreat. He connected a road from his residence to the main Belfast–Dublin Road, so that his journeys to and from Dublin avoided the town of Newry. (It is difficult nowadays to imagine the challenges of those regular return journeys to and from Dublin by coach and horses over roads that at times must have been merely passable.)

Corry sold the house in 1810 and retired to his home in Dublin where he died in 1813 aged sixty. The building was bought by John Grubb Richardson in 1859, and shortly after the Second World War the Richardson family donated the house to the National Trust. It was first opened to the general public in 1957.

I never saw inside Derrymore House, as it was then called, during my boyhood in Bessbrook, because it was closed for many years. Therefore it is no surprise that I, and many others like me, did not appreciate its Irish historical significance. In fact, one of my long-abiding memories of my days in Bessbrook was not of travelling across the Irish border to visit Dundalk or Dublin, but rather of going to Belfast with thousands of other Cub Scouts to Balmoral Showgrounds to see the newly crowned Queen Elizabeth II and the Duke of Edinburgh.

It is important to underline, however, that my sense of being British and Unionist was the exact opposite of the Catholic children of the village who were brought up, with some exceptions, to regard themselves as Irish and Nationalist. I had no opportunity to find out what their education was like, but I was told later on that the stern principal of the Catholic boys' primary school, a man called Pappy Fearon, was a strong Irish Nationalist. In earlier times he had been an accomplished Gaelic player who had participated in Armagh County's victory in their 1926 Junior All-Ireland GAA Championship success. He also served as County Secretary from 1925–29, and had the honour of captaining the county team.[3]

While Fearon educated the boys in the primary school near the chapel, the girls went to school at the convent, and those were tough times. A lady called Annie Moan remembered walking up the big hill to the convent school in her bare feet, and that the nuns who taught her were very strict. The school day began with morning prayers and hymn-singing, followed by Catechism lessons, and then writing, spelling and arithmetic. There were no lay teachers, only nuns. There were also classes for boys, but they were held in a different part of the convent.

This huge divide in education invariably maintained the divisions in society later on, with appalling consequences, but this division was a reflection of the lack of cooperation in both parts of Ireland in those days. When King George V opened the Northern Ireland parliament in 1921, he made the heartfelt appeal 'to all Irishmen to pause, to stretch out the hand of forbearance and conciliation, to forgive and to forget, and to join in making for the land which they love a new era of peace, contentment and good will'.[4]

Sadly, this was not to be. Northern Ireland and the Irish Republic became separate entities in an atmosphere of mutual distrust. The cultural chasm between North and South was highlighted by quotes from two prominent men on each side of the border. On 24 April 1934, during a debate in the Northern Ireland parliament, Prime Minister James Craig stated, 'They still boast of Southern Ireland being a Catholic State ... we are a Protestant Parliament and a Protestant State.'[5] Ten years later the Catholic Archbishop of Dublin, John Charles McQuaid, stated, 'No Catholic may enter the Protestant University of Trinity College without the previous permission of the ordinary of the Diocese. Any Catholic who disobeys this is guilty of mortal sin, and while he persists in disobedience, is unworthy to receive the sacraments.'[6]

Craig had spoken his words six years before I was born, and McQuaid when I was only four. Given the prevailing sectarianism in both parts of Ireland at that time, what chance did young people like me have of being involved with integrated education or of getting to know 'the other side' from an early age? Integration would not have solved all the problems of inter-community tensions and mistrust, but it would have gone a considerable way towards doing so. Integrated education began to be established in the North during the worst of the Troubles, and in the following decades. To many people on both sides this was a welcome development, but it was at least fifty years too late.

At the age of twelve, I passed the Eleven-Plus examination to gain entrance to Newry Grammar School, which opened the way for me to aspire to the dizzy heights of a university education. My primary school teacher, James Darragh, was not sure that I would pass the exam, nor was I, because I had no idea what it meant. However, Mr Darragh persevered with me, and despite the tough treatment in his classroom at times, I owe him a great debt for literally hammering into me the rules of English grammar, thus providing me with the basics to pursue a professional career as a writer.

It would be good if I could state that I found grammar school education exciting and challenging, but in reality I felt bewildered and intimidated at the start. I was burdened by a large satchel of books, and because I was the first in my family to go to a grammar school there was no one at home who could help me with my studies if a problem arose. I remember walking over a mile and back on a cold winter's night to seek help from a fellow pupil when I had a problem with mathematics, which was not my strong subject. However, I survived, for there was no alternative, and I remember being befriended during my early schooldays in Newry by a lovely girl called Arlene. It was only decades later that I found out that she was my cousin. Her mother was the sister of my absent father Norman.

For the first time I was attending a mixed school. However, in the early days at Newry Grammar I hardly noticed the other sex. Girls were part of a world unknown to me, and I am quite sure that they felt the same about the boys.

Ours was a solid though unfashionable country school, but we had teachers who did their best for us. I was particularly indebted to Miss Ethel Meneely, my English teacher, who spotted my fluency in writing early on and gave me the confidence to believe in myself at a time when I was struggling painfully with the perceived stigma of being born out of wedlock.

My history teacher, Johnny Spence, also gave me great help. He was a tense and peppery little man who taught history almost by rote to the point where I passed my A-levels in that subject with a high mark of 84 per cent. It was only when I began to study history at Queen's University that I realised I had to learn to study it for myself. I read British, European and Commonwealth history, but I have no recollection of studying Irish history at school or, perhaps more accurately, of reading history from an Irish point of view.

The gap between the two cultures was evident outside our school. There were several Catholic grammar schools in Newry, but because we were based in different parts of the town, we never met as pupils. The educational apartheid of the primary system was being continued, yet we never complained or thought that this was odd. They were Catholics and we were Protestants, and we could never meet. This seemed perfectly normal to us, in our abnormality.

Nevertheless, there was one notable exception outside school hours. Sport was always a great unifying influence. I became the goalie for a Bessbrook youth soccer team called Evergreen, which had Catholic and Protestant members. It was here that I got to know a young Catholic called Graham McAleer, and we became lifelong friends, together with a Protestant youth called Morris Brown, who was a member of my wider family.

Our team played in a competition in Newry, apparently staged to help pay for a new Catholic chapel in the town. We narrowly won the final game, during which I was greatly impressed by the skill of the opposing goalie. After the match ended, I said to him, 'You played a blinder, son – what's your name?' He replied, 'Pat Jennings'. Neither of us knew then that he would become argu-ably the best goalie ever in the Northern Ireland soccer team, and in his prime he was one of the best in the world. I always resist the temptation to boast wrongly that as a goalie myself I taught Pat all about the basics of good goalkeeping!

Religious education (RE) was compulsory in Newry Grammar School but an RE session was regarded by our unruly class as a welcome break from other more challenging subjects and teachers. Lessons on comparative religions and multi-faith societies were unheard of. Our RE teacher was a Presbyterian minister, the Reverend Victor Henderson from Rostrevor, who tried earnestly to pass on some spiritual wisdom to our class, which had little or no interest in religion.

I was impressed by the fact that 'Hendy' had been an Irish international table tennis player, which was much more interesting to me than his clerical dog collar. Sometimes I asked him to explain to me some 'simple' problems, such as the meaning of life, but I soon realised that there was no simple answer to such a profound mystery. I respected him greatly, however, because he did not try to answer my questions with religious clichés like 'You must be born again.' Instead he encouraged me to try to work out things for myself.

Mr Henderson was a jolly and friendly man who also tried valiantly to make us learn by heart a series of well-known biblical passages. I only ever remembered the striking words from Isaiah 40: '... but those who wait for the Lord shall renew their strength; they shall mount up with wings like eagles; they shall run and not be weary; they shall walk and not faint.' This quotation seemed nonsensical to me in my callow youth; many decades later I realised that it was spiritually comforting, especially in those times when life was difficult and it was not easy to know where to turn. No doubt 'Hendy' has already entered the great table tennis stadium in the sky, but I daresay he would be pleased if he knew that at least one of the pearls of spiritual wisdom that he tried to impart to me still shines brightly and helpfully in my inner life so many years later.

I have another warm memory of Victor Henderson, which has nothing to do with learning biblical passages. At Newry Grammar I was good at hockey and eventually I was picked to play for the Ulster Schoolboys team. This was a great boost to my self-confidence, and when I was chosen to take part in a trial game in Dublin for the Ireland boys' side I was even more delighted.

This was something beyond my wildest dreams, even though the match was eventually rained off at the last moment. I didn't get my Irish cap, which went to the Dublin goalie-in-residence. I comfort myself by rationalising that in modern times I would be chosen for the Irish squad, which would have more than one goalkeeper.

One Saturday morning, before all this unfolded, I was waiting for a lift from Newry to Dublin from the father and uncle of another Ireland schoolboy hockey player who, like me, was travelling to the trial venue. I saw Mr Henderson coming to meet me. He had travelled from Rostrevor to wish me well before we drove off. He did not have to do that, but his thoughtful gesture was a comfort to me at a time when I needed a boost to my confidence for such an important sporting challenge.

That made me realise that what people actually do, or fail to do, is what counts. Mere words, biblical or otherwise, are often not worth taking seriously. The Reverend Victor Henderson was good with words, but he was even better at bringing encouragement and comfort to young people who needed a kind word, or, to put it another way, at practising what he preached.

At the end of my six years at Newry Grammar School I did well enough, with an average of over 60 per cent in three A levels, to win an education scholarship to Queen's University.

I was excited that a new adventure was about to begin, and above all that I would be leaving Bessbrook for a future career that would be much more promising than a job in the local mill. I was also apprehensive about this brave new world that I was about to enter, but I realised that there could, and would, be no turning back. As I sat on a bus trundling north from Newry with nearly all my worldly belongings crammed into a large suitcase, I wondered what life would be like for me in the big, bustling and tough city of Belfast. I knew that I would find that out all too soon.

4

Brave New World

My five years at the Queen's University, from 1959–64, were some of the most formative of my life. There was no sense of formal religion, such as going to church regularly, but I did keep in touch with the Presbyterian Centre at Queen's, and occasionally I attended services at the fashionable Fisherwick Presbyterian Church on the upmarket Malone Road.

However, while my main interests were elsewhere, I met some people from a faith background who influenced me. I also realised much later that a university education at its best was not only gaining a degree, but also acquiring the discipline of 'learning to learn'. This was a phrase that I often used when helping to write the speeches for Queen's Vice-Chancellor Sir Gordon Beveridge when I was Head of Information at the university some thirty years later.

I read modern history but I made little time for academic work. There were times after I left Queen's when I was tempted to work for a master's degree or a PhD, but I was aware that the vast amount of that research, carried out while writing several big books, including the history of the Harbour Commissioners in Belfast and the history of the Royal College of Physicians of Ireland in Dublin, would have been more than enough for several post-graduate degrees.

I also realised that I would not have had the patience or time to adapt my writing style to a strict academic discipline. When one of my tutors marked my essay 'Good, but tends to journalese', I rejoiced. To be honest, I should have learned more about history during my time at university, but I learned a great deal about life.

Belfast in the Swinging Sixties was an exciting city. It was relatively peaceful, and there was an air of optimism about the place. At eighteen it seemed to me that anything was possible, and that the violence of earlier generations, which had disfigured the face of Ireland, was over. We had survived the sporadic and dangerous border war between the IRA and the security forces in the fifties – there were people in Bessbrook who had taken up arms on both sides. When I went up to Queen's that seemed to be over, and I thought that I was entering a brave new world.

In some ways I was right, and I enjoyed the start of the last few years of comparative peace before we were all engulfed by decades of fierce conflict, as militant Republicans and Loyalists fought with each other and with the police and army in a fierce battle to attack or to protect the constitutional position of Northern Ireland as part of the UK. It was also a battle for the soul of a province where so many people in the early sixties had looked for light and hope and progress, but were all too soon plunged into a pervasive darkness.

During my first few weeks at Queen's, I was excited by the cosmopolitan character of the university. There were students from all over Northern Ireland and other parts of the UK, and far beyond that. There was one particularly striking blond German called Jürgen. I had never even seen a real German until then.

My awareness of Germany had been confined to the annual Remembrance Day services at the Charlemont Square Cenotaph in Bessbrook, where my grandfather, who had fought Germans in the First World War, stood stiffly beside his ex-service colleagues to pay tribute to their fallen comrades. Yet here at Queen's was a young student whose grandfather might well have fought on the German side in the same war.

This possibility widened my horizons greatly. In my first year I won my place in the university's First XI hockey team, which took part in a tournament in Essen, where we played against some crack sides, including a champion team called Berliner. To my amazement our game was broadcast live on German radio. One or two years later our team also visited Hamburg, which gave me further exposure to German sport and culture.

One of the most memorable visits of all was when I played for the British Universities XI against the West German Universities XI in Munich. Hockey was an upmarket sport in Germany and, as I walked down the stairs of the impressive clubhouse on my way to the pitch, I noticed a large war memorial with the names of many Germans who had died in two world wars. The realisation that the Germans had also suffered horrendous casualties stopped me in my tracks. I recognised that there was another side to the story of the conflict, as well as the 1955 film about the 'heroic' Dam Busters, or the 'courageous' Allied prisoners depicted in *The Great Escape* movie, which was released just a year before I visited Munich.

I had come a long way from my little village in South Armagh, and it took me a long time afterwards to realise that all this was happening to me at Queen's less than twenty years after Hitler had committed suicide in his Berlin bunker in 1945. As you get older, your awareness of history telescopes from being a broad view of a distant past, into a very personal experience through which you lived and breathed at first hand.

My time at Queen's widened my horizon in other ways. There were only some 3,000 students around the campus at that time, compared to nearly 25,000 today.[7] This meant that there was much more opportunity to meet new people. The canteen in the small but atmospheric Students' Union was a great focal point, but in the early days some Protestants and Catholics sat at separate tables because they played different sports – rugby and hockey were mainly 'Protestant', while Gaelic football and camogie were traditionally 'Catholic'.

Fortunately there was still a lot of mixing, and the 'craic' was good. There was also great mixing in the Old Library, where there was often much more talking than studying. At the student dances or 'hops' there was another special experience that crossed the barriers. When Protestants and Catholics danced with each other no one cared about their religious backgrounds. It was a case of 'boy meets girl,' or, sometimes more realistically, 'boy hopes to meet girl', and vice versa.

I don't know how I managed to pass my first-year exams, as I had studied so little, but I was accepted in my second year for the Honours School in the Department of Modern History. This was a further three-year course, which bound me tightly into a small mixed group of eight people.

They included Austin Currie, who later became a prominent politician North and South, and a lifelong friend whose courage I admired greatly. Harry Uprichard became Presbyterian Moderator many years later, and Ronnie Spence was later a top civil servant. Another colleague was called Dymphna, and there was Seamus from Derry. These were names that I had not encountered in Newry Grammar School but at Queen's no one bothered about such things.

We had worked hard to reach the high academic admission standards required for entry, and were, by and large, the first scholarship students from our families to be able to attend university. Our tuition fees were paid by the government, and we seemed to have a bright future. We did not realise then that we were a gilded generation, compared to later students who had to mix with much larger numbers at university, who did not have their fees paid and who in many cases found it difficult to get a job once they graduated.

We in the History Department were also fortunate in having excellent teachers, some of whom, like Professors Michael Roberts and Lewis Warren, were world-class experts in their special subjects. Professor Warren was particularly helpful in assisting me to catch up with my studies, which I had partly ignored due to other self-made pressures. He once said to me, 'The more simple societies seem, the more complex they are likely to be.' He also taught me that in good writing 'less is more'. He once told my class,

'Mr McCreary writes a good essay, but only after the twenty-first page.' I didn't like to hear that, but he was right.

J. C. Beckett, a small, charming and eccentric academic, was the highly regarded Professor of Irish History. He encouraged us to make up our own minds about the complex history of Ireland and to learn to separate truth from myth and fiction. I will always remember his summary of Ireland past and present. He said, 'The real border is not on the landscape of Ireland, it is the border in people's minds.' Those words ring as true to me today as when I heard them over fifty years ago.

Outside the lectures and tutorials, the bustling life of Queen's continued apace, and there were many individuals who went on to make their names in different ways. A few years ahead of me was Seamus Heaney, a brilliant poet and a decent human being who had no airs or graces, and Robin Eames, a law student who became an outstanding Church of Ireland primate and at one stage was on the shortlist for archbishop of Canterbury.

My contemporaries also included Phil Coulter, who had an amazingly successful career as a musician and songwriter, and who carried his great musical talent and success lightly. He was deservedly awarded an honorary degree by Queen's and later the freedom of his native Derry. He, too, remained a lifelong friend. Geoffrey Martin, another lifelong friend from Bessbrook, who was part of my wider family on my father's side, became President of the National Union of Students. Later on he was the first Head of the European Office in Northern Ireland, and had several years as Head of the Representation of the European Commission in the UK, based in London.

Geoff shared my feeling of wonder at finding himself at Queen's. He once said to me, 'As a boy I felt safe in my home in Cromie Place, with the mill horn sounding over the village, the Presbyterian church just down the road from me, and the beautiful Camlough Mountain in the near distance.

'In school we learned about the English kings and queens, and we sang "Land of Hope and Glory", which seemed so powerful.

The Bible was omnipresent, but there was no mention of Catholics. The first Catholic I ever met was Austin Currie. That was only in my late teens when I went up to Queen's, and we became a lifelong friends. I realised that a new world was opening up.'

It seemed like that to most of us. There was so much talent and synergy between Catholics and Protestants at Queen's, which could have enabled us to enter the world outside and to begin to build a new and tolerant society for everyone, to banish violence and discord to the distant past. Tragically, that did not happen. It was a lost opportunity, seemingly gone for ever.

Perhaps we were naive to expect that the rival Unionists and Irish Nationalists and tribes outside the walls of academe would take down their tents and steal away quietly into the undergrowth of their disputed history. Few of us were keeping an eye on the political realities outside the campus, which was dominated by the beautiful Lanyon Building, designed in 1845 by the celebrated architect Sir Charles Lanyon and said to have been modelled on Magdalen College Oxford.

Those of us who expected better things for Northern Ireland from the sixties onwards did not realise that the meeting of many minds at Queen's was not reflected in what was happening in the housing estates, towns, cities and villages of rural Ulster, where people were clinging to the old attitudes and prejudices.

The Reverend Ian Paisley, the hard-line Protestant politician and preacher who invented his own Church and political party – and perhaps even his own version of God – was already on the rampage through the cities, towns and countryside of Northern Ireland, but we did not notice what was going on. A colleague in my Queen's class told me one night of attending a Paisley rally in the Ulster Hall during which he was involved in an altercation and had his shirt collar torn off. We thought that that this was funny, because Paisley was regarded by us as a rabble-rousing joke. Unfortunately, we did not look up to see the looming dark war clouds.

For most of us at Queen's, religion was a label that was rarely, if ever, mentioned. When I went to church it was usually to help to put in the morning of a Belfast Sunday, when nothing else was open, and there was little else to do. The Belfast Sunday was not quite as bad as some of its critics remembered, but it bore no resemblance to the events-packed Sundays in the lively city of today.

I went to Fisherwick Presbyterian Church occasionally, partly because I admired the eloquence of its minister, the Reverend Jack Withers. I was in awe of a speaker like Withers who could command a pulpit with his delivery, and even broadcast 'live' on BBC Radio, apparently effortlessly.

Yet even when I sat listening to him preach about the Good News, I also had pangs of guilt as I remembered drinking pints of great Guinness the night before in the Botanic Inn just across the road. One Sunday evening I went to the Presbyterian Centre to hear Jack Withers give a talk to students, and when he had finished, he lit up a cigarette and started smoking. I was completely shocked, because where I came from, a Presbyterian minister certainly did not smoke. I was not as liberal as I had thought.

I went to the Presbyterian Centre for the first time only a few days after I had settled in to my lodgings in Belfast at the start of the first term. I went there not necessarily to talk to other Presbyterians but to meet new people in a big city that was overwhelming to a boy from the country. I was introduced to the university's Presbyterian chaplain, the Reverend Ray Davey. He was a welcoming man with a warm smile and a firm handshake, and while he was open and considerate he also had an air of quiet inner peace and authority.

The Presbyterian Centre was not at the top of my list of priorities but I went there on a few occasions, usually during the long boring winter Sunday evenings in Belfast, and I met other students who had gone there, like me, for something to do. Our visits, however, were not boring, and I was attracted by Ray's friendly presence as he chatted to us after the guest speaker had left the stage.

At other times during the week I dropped in to the centre for a coffee with Ray and his warm-hearted wife Kathleen. They were good listeners and great company. I never felt that I was visiting the Presbyterian chaplain and his wife, but just meeting friends. Ray did not talk much about himself, but I gradually I heard part of his impressive back story. He had volunteered for service during the Second World War, during which he had been a field worker with the YMCA and the Allied Forces in the African Desert War.

He had been captured after the fall of Tobruk by German troops led by Field-Marshal Rommel and had been incarcerated in Italian and German prisoner-of-war camps. During this harsh confinement he had realised the need to create and maintain good relations among the Allied prisoners who had no prospect of an early release, and were deeply dispirited and frustrated.

Ray also talked to me about the importance of his Christian faith, not in a preachy way but in a manner that made sense to me. He saw the urgent need to create wider and better community relations in Northern Ireland, where the divisions were all too apparent. He was light years ahead of most of his contemporaries in foreseeing this need.

His vision was based not on political expediency or sociological experimentation but on the core principles of the Gospel message. He did not make this sound holy, but rather as an obvious need to build bridges in the wider community and to prevent the conflict that would surely come if those bridges were not built.

The Unionists and Nationalists were still parading behind their banners and flags and their flute bands, pipe bands and accordion bands, and celebrating the battles and other events of the past. Ray Davey was looking to the future, and he was walking to the beat of a different drum.

I came to realise that I too wanted to walk to that same drum-beat in my own way, but that it would require the right time and right opportunity for me to do so. I had a hunch that such a time might come, even if I did not know when or where, but I knew that it was certainly not just yet.

5

Headlines and Deadlines

When John E. Sayers, Editor-in-Chief of the *Belfast Telegraph*, offered me a job as a journalist in June 1964, I felt as if all my birthdays and Christmas Days had been rolled into one. In the previous year, because of my sporting record at Queen's, I had been asked to write an article on sport for the Students Union magazine.

After completing that article I had a 'Damascus Road' moment, because I knew that this was something I wanted to do for the rest of my professional life. The problem was that I did not know how to break into journalism, and that, in itself, was my first big challenge. When the parents of aspiring journalists ask me how their son or daughter might or could become a journalist, I usually reply, 'If a young person lacks the compulsion and initiative to break into journalism in the first place, he or she is unlikely to make a success of it anyway.' My rocky path from studying history at Queen's to becoming a professional journalist is a story in itself.

In the final year of my course, I became painfully aware that I had not done nearly enough work during the previous three years, and this developed into a scramble, then a panic and ultimately a nightmare as the final examinations loomed. However, I must have learned more than I had realised, as I emerged from Queen's with a respectable Honours BA in Modern History. The nightmares lasted for years afterwards.

I had a degree but no job. Earlier I had attended an interview at the *Belfast Telegraph*, and a slick executive from London later offered me a job as an advertising salesman. This was something I did not want, even though I thought that perhaps I might be transferred later from selling advertising to writing for the paper. That would definitely not have happened, so I obeyed my original instinct and bravely turned down the offer.

Unlike some of my contemporaries who had the prospect of a lucrative career in law or medicine, I had nothing to look forward to. Fortunately, I had good friends, and when I was working as a temporary bus conductor in the seaside town of Eastbourne in Sussex, my old pal Geoff Martin helped to sort things out during his visit there to see a friend.

We decided that the best way to break into journalism was to return to Queen's and to take a post-graduate course, which would give me time to build up my experience as a writer. This is exactly what I did, and almost miraculously the path opened up. I was awarded a teacher-training scholarship, even though I had applied for this long after the closing date, and I joined the student newspaper *Gown* as their sports editor.

Within a short period the editor of *Gown* had printed two stories that brought threats of libel writs, and the financially troubled paper was in danger of folding. All the student staff resigned, apart from me, because I could see a way forward. With the help of others we raised money from an appeal for financial help from the entire student body for an indemnity fund, and *Gown* survived.

This gave me a year in student journalism, but again at the cost of neglecting my studies. Halfway through the course I was summoned to the study of the overbearing Professor of Education, Harry Knox ,who ranted about my poor attendance record at his lectures. I decided to try to charm the man, and agreed with him that I had indeed been a poor student. To his surprise I told him the true story that I had a teaching job lined up in Kenya, and that I needed my diploma in education to take it up.

Having almost exhausted himself in tearing me apart verbally, he began to mellow and suggested that I might scrape through if I started to work at my education course. I learned from this encounter the truth of the old biblical maxim that 'a soft answer turns away wrath', but it was only later that I realised that Professor Knox had done me a favour in making me change my ways.

If he had not intervened I might have left Queen's without my diploma in education and possibly with a large bill for the repayment of my fees. I had long thought of Knox as a bumptious and irascible academic who had enjoyed giving me a grilling and was best ignored, but he was perhaps more helpful than I had thought. I now realise that I owe him a debt of gratitude for helping to straighten me out, and regrettably this is something of which I was not aware until quite recently.

Towards the end of my diploma year, I decided to make a final effort to get a job in journalism by writing directly to J. E. Sayers at the *Belfast Telegraph*. To my great surprise, he granted me an interview, and we met at the end of his working afternoon. Initially it did not go well. Sayers asked me if I had gone to the prestigious Campbell College grammar school, which some people said had the cream of male pupils because a number of them were rich and thick. No, I had not gone to Campbell but to the relatively unknown Newry Grammar School; no, I had not played 'rugger', but had made my name in the unfashionable sport of men's hockey.

As we talked I sensed that the conversation was not going my way. So I played my final card and told Sayers how I had led a team that had rescued the student newspaper *Gown*, which I had then edited for the rest of the year. He showed a deep interest in this, and eventually offered me a job on the spot. Those were the days when powerful editors could do that kind of thing, without having to go through the modern hoops of human resources and other administrative procedures.

I accepted Sayers's offer enthusiastically, and left his office walking on air. I knew that this appointment was a major step forward for me in my career, but I did not realise until many years later that Jack Sayers was not only a remarkable editor but that he had a distinguished war record and a deep religious faith that had sustained him and underpinned his visionary policy of bridge-building in a divided society.

My first years in the *Belfast Telegraph* were an exciting whirl. After attending the first graduate journalist's training course in the London School of Economics I joined the *Telegraph* newsroom to work with my colleagues, who had mostly trained in the provincial weeklies before obtaining a job at the Belfast newspaper.

There was a certain wariness among some colleagues about these newfangled graduates taking journalists' jobs, but once I showed that I could spell and write good copy, I became part of a team with some very good journalists, who honed their reputation in the *Telegraph* and later went on to higher things.

Of course I had early challenges and setbacks, but after one lean spell, I remember Deputy Chief Sub-Editor Tommy Edgar taking me aside and saying quietly, 'Young man, you wrote an excellent piece for us yesterday. Keep it up.' His kind words went a long way, and during my career I made a point of doing the same for other journalists who deserved a word of praise. Sadly that seems to happen less often nowadays.

John E. Sayers, known to his close associates as 'Jack' and to the rest of us as 'JES', was a formidable figure who kept a strict eye on every aspect of the paper. He was smallish in stature and not particularly prepossessing physically, but he had an immense presence that could fill a room. He was one of the last great 'writing' editors and one of the best in the history of the *Belfast Telegraph*.

He could be quite aloof, and in reality I was in awe of him. He was like a faintly distant headmaster whose word was law, but he spoke with authority. He was the third generation of the Sayers family to edit the paper, had learned his journalism from the bottom up, and had a distinguished career outside journalism before he took over the paper.

JES had followed the naval tradition of his family, joining the Royal Navy Volunteer Reserve shortly before the outbreak of the Second World War, during which he saw active service. He was on board the HMS *Courageous* in an Atlantic convoy when it was torpedoed in 1939 by a German U-boat. It sank swiftly but he managed to escape, and after some time in the cold ocean he was picked up by an American merchant vessel. Out of a crew of 1,260, as many as 518 drowned, including the captain.[8]

Later on Sayers worked in the Winston Churchill Map Room, which plotted the course of the Second World War. He spent six years there, and Churchill described him as 'the Ulsterman with the Card Index memory'. He became known as 'The Indexer'.[9] After the war he was apparently offered a job in the *Daily Telegraph*, but turned it down to return to Belfast to pursue his career in the paper that was so close to him.

When I worked for Jack Sayers in the mid-sixties I was not aware of his impressive record. In reality I was trying to stay on his good side while learning at speed how to become a journalist. I knew that Jack had favourite subjects, which included Queen's University, Harland and Wolff, the shipbuilders, and all things naval. These were subjects about which you wrote at your peril because Jack read every word in the paper.

He also had a sharp tongue when he was annoyed. One morning I was struggling with a complicated story about the Methodist Church, with red warning lights in my mind, when suddenly Jack strode in to the big open newsroom and yelled at me, 'You should be covering the military march past at the City Hall by the Royal Ulster Rifles, so what are you doing here in the office?' My simple answer was that I could not be in two places at once, but I did not dare speak back to Jack Sayers in full flow. Fortunately the Assistant News Editor, Cecil Deeny, an excellent journalist and a good man, caught my eye as if to say, 'Don't worry son, I understand your predicament.' I breathed a huge sigh of relief as I finished my Methodist Church story, and headed for the military parade which, to be fair to Sayers, was an important historic occasion that needed to be reported.

Jack, in his own way, was considerate and helpful, and his occasional small note of praise, written and signed 'JES', was always treasured. I was also aware of his foibles. For example he was class-conscious – he once sent me to interview someone he described as 'a member of the lesser gentry'.

Jack was born in 1911, and he was a man of this time, but I am forever grateful to have been spotted, trained and appreciated by an editor of such eminence and with such a strong inner life and faith.

Though my later years in the *Belfast Telegraph* were spent in its higher editorial echelons, my early days were spent as a reporter during what was a 'normal' period in Ulster life, with a stability that seemed destined never to return.

I had no real appreciation of the fact that I had graduated very quickly from a short career in student journalism to work for a daily evening paper which had a circulation of 200,000 and which was read in Protestant and Catholic homes all over the province.

Ulster Television was established in 1959 and five years later I was appointed as the television critic of our sister sports-paper, *Ireland's Saturday Night*. This opened doors for me in ITV and the BBC, and also gave me a chance to write and to comment on a wide range of subjects.

There was an air of optimism about the place. The IRA's border war of the 1950s had ended in failure, there was a great deal of inward investment bringing new prosperity and much-needed jobs. Significantly there was a new prime minister, Captain Terence O'Neill, who was willing to stretch his hand of friendship across the divides. His predecessor, Lord Brookeborough, by contrast, was an old-fashioned 'No Surrender' Unionist.

There was one important difference, however. Brookeborough, despite his background of 'The Big House', had a folksy charm, and he could talk easily to his supporters about all aspects of farming and of Orange politics. O'Neill was a shy man, and his background of Eton and the Irish Guards was far removed from the rank-and-file Unionists of the mid-sixties.

O'Neill also had an unfortunate habit of referring to 'Londondree', instead of the more common 'Londonderry' or 'Derry'. This jarred in the ears of Unionists and Nationalists alike, and rein-forced the feeling that this well-meaning man was still somewhat of a stranger in our midst.

It was clear, however, that he had considerable political cour-age, and in January 1965 he invited Irish Taoiseach Seán Lemass, a veteran of the 1916 Rising in Dublin, for secret talks at the Stormont headquarters of the Northern Ireland government. This was a visionary and much-needed attempt to establish better rela-tions between Dublin and Belfast, which had been extremely frosty from as far back as the Partition of Ireland over forty years previously.

However, O'Neill made a major political mistake in not telling the majority of his Unionist colleagues about the proposed visit, and political uproar ensued. Paisley was told about the visit while Lemass was still at the talks, and he rushed with his noisy sup-porters to Stormont to confront the Taoiseach.

They were too late to make a significant impact, but they showed their fury by throwing verbal abuse and snowballs at the limou-sine carrying Lemass as it drove through the Stormont gates and sped on its way back to Dublin.

I witnessed this at first hand, because I was already at a boring planning appeal in a Stormont committee room, far removed from the part of the building where the O'Neill–Lemass talks were taking place. Someone had tipped off the *Belfast Telegraph* and the news editor urgently contacted me to ask for a report on the Paisley protest, but it was all but over by the time I got there.

However, it was an ugly scene and a portent of things to come. For a young journalist like me it was exciting to have my first close view of history in the making, but it was also a wake-up call to remind me and others that Paisley was not the joke figure we had imagined. He was becoming a serious threat to the bridge-building efforts of Terence O'Neill. I was all too soon aware that there was a fierce struggle taking place for the very soul of North-ern Ireland, and that this was symbolised by the involvement of three influential men in particular – Terence O'Neill, Ian Paisley, and Jack Sayers of the *Belfast Telegraph*.

From the very start of his premiership Terence O'Neill was determined to drag his Unionist Party away from the uncompromising attitudes of the past, and to work for a future where Catholics would feel welcomed and secure in a Unionist-dominated Northern Ireland, and where they would have equal opportunities in jobs and housing. He also saw that a stable and secure Northern Ireland would attract even more investment and that the province could become a model of a form of devolved government within the UK. He also was adamant that better relations between Northern Ireland and the Irish Republic were vitally important at a time when horizons were broadening in Dublin and elsewhere.

O'Neill was also aware that young Ulster Catholics with the benefit of a good secondary and third-level education would be equipped to campaign vociferously for their rights, and that the Unionist-dominated government needed not only to be aware of this but also to be prepared to do something about it.

He did not just talk about what needed to be done, he also led by example. He visited Catholic schools and hospitals, and stated in his autobiography, '… Not only were the people in these schools and hospitals delighted to see me, but they also noted that I came among them, as I went everywhere in Northern Ireland, without a detective, or indeed protection of any kind.'[10]

He also noted tartly that his next two successors to the Unionist leadership 'could have benefitted from the ice-breaking precedent which I had created, by visiting Catholic schools and Catholic hospitals, but they were too frightened of offending their Protestant followers. I am not conscious that I ever saw of photograph of either of them in the company of a priest or a nun.'[11]

O'Neill had some success in trying to build up a Unionist middle ground but he was facing the sectarian demons of the past, which found fresh energy and strident new voices, and which put obstacles in the path of all the major attempts to cross the sectarian divides. The outcome of this political drama between progress and 'No Surrender' would determine the future of Northern Ireland and its people for decades to come. At one crucial point, O'Neill gave a brilliant televised address to all the people, asking them bluntly ,'What kind of Ulster do you want?'; in other words, 'Do you want peace, prosperity and progress, or do you want to slide back into the worst of the past with its violence and discord?' Sadly, we found out the answer all too soon.

6

The Storm Clouds Gather

Much has been written already about the life and career of the Reverend Ian Paisley, who was coming to prominence in the early 1960s, around the same time that I was learning my profession as a young journalist in the *Belfast Telegraph*, which he loathed, and which was totally opposed to almost everything he stood for.

One of the fascinations and problems for a journalist working in historic times is that while you are living through constant uncertainty and upheaval, you have no idea as to how that historical process will unfold. In reality you have more than enough to write and think about every day.

In my university days, Paisley had seemed a comical and remote street preacher in the undergrowth of Protestant fundamentalism, but as the storm clouds gathered over the sunny skies of the Unionists' all-too-brief experiment in liberalism and bridge-building, he demonstrated a remarkable ability to grab the headlines at crucial moments. This gave him a profile that at times was higher even than the prime minister of Northern Ireland or any of the government ministers and politicians at Stormont.

In this respect he was similar to US President Donald J. Trump, whose strident demagoguery mesmerised millions of Republicans by pandering to their deepest-held fears and by promising them something that they wished would happen, but which to others appeared unachievable. He promised to 'Make America Great', but in reality he made it worse.

Ian Paisley, many decades earlier, had reassured his ultra-Protestant supporters that God was on their side, and despite the best intentions of Unionist visionaries like O'Neill, he convinced them that Loyal Ulster would never abandon its mantra of 'No Surrender' and allow itself to be dragged under the false banner of civil rights into a 'Papist and priest-ridden' Irish Republic. Against all the signs to the contrary, they believed him.

Paisley, the son of an independent Baptist minister, was born in Armagh in 1926 and brought up in the Ballymena Bible Belt area. He gained an early reputation as a firebrand and eloquent evangelical preacher, and in 1951 he formed his own Free Presbyterian Church, which was totally out of sympathy with the more broad-based, more liberal Presbyterian Church, the largest Protestant denomination in Northern Ireland.

Paisley really began to make headlines after the death of Pope John XXIII on 3 June 1963. Condolences were sent to Rome on behalf of all the people of Northern Ireland by the governor, Lord Wakehurst. Prime Minister Terence O'Neill said that the late pope 'had won widespread acclaim throughout the world because of his qualities of kindness and humanity'. The flag on Belfast City Hall was flown at half-mast, an important symbolic tribute to the late pontiff in a city with varied political aspirations.

By contrast, Paisley told a packed audience in the nearby Ulster Hall, 'This Romish man of sin is now in Hell.'[12] Apart from his astonishing theological arrogance in claiming that he knew what God's judgement would be on another departed human being, it was an offensive remark made in extremely bad taste. Yet it was not surprising. Paisley was a ruthless past master at grabbing a headline, and he was a genius of the sound bite long before that term had become popular.

Meanwhile, the dark clouds were gathering ever more ominously as O'Neill was bravely trying to cross the divides, which none of his Unionist forebears had even attempted to do. In 1964 there were riots in Belfast's Divis Street when Paisley threatened to remove an Irish tricolour flag being flown 'illegally' from

Republican headquarters in West Belfast, thus forcing the police to intervene. Reports of violence in Belfast were now competing for headlines with good news stories about inward investment.

The year 1966 was particularly significant, with the murder of a Catholic, Peter Ward, by militant Loyalists in Malvern Street, Belfast. In the same year the revival of the Ulster Volunteer Force as a new paramilitary group began to take shape, alongside the emergence of several organisations that led to the establishment of the civil rights movement.

Undaunted, Paisley continued on his mission to maintain his high profile and to boost his 'O'Neill must go' campaign. On 6 June 1966 he and his followers marched past Republican territory in the Markets area of Belfast and on to the city centre to protest at the alleged 'Romanising' tendencies of the Presbyterian Church. The locals attacked the marchers, who were singing 'Onward Christian Soldiers', with bricks and other missiles, and the police were caught in the middle, not for the first or last time.

Once at the city centre, Paisley and his acolytes marched around City Hall three times before confronting the guests at the opening night of the Presbyterian Church's General Assembly, including the then Governor of Northern Ireland, Lord Erskine, and his wife who, with others at the Assembly, were vilified with accusations of 'Popehead' and 'Romanist'.[13]

Throwing down this gauntlet was a direct challenge to the Presbyterian Church on the evening of one of the most treasured ceremonies in its annual calendar. It was also an attack on Lord Erskine, who had intervened earlier that year to force the renaming of a major new landmark across the River Lagan as the 'Queen Elizabeth II Bridge', rather than the 'Carson Bridge', which the Unionist-dominated Belfast City Council had unwisely and not unsurprisingly chosen earlier in honour of one of the founders of Unionism. It was also an attack on the queen's representative, and a carefully calculated insult to the Westminster government.

The incident, which was widely publicised in all the media, shocked the hundreds of members of the Presbyterian Assembly who had gathered from congregations all over Ireland to attend the annual event at Church House. They were also greatly embarrassed that Lady Erskine had been severely shaken by the disturbance, and required medical treatment two days later. No one had experienced anything like it in the decades since Northern Ireland was established. Up to that time such a display of bully-boy tactics and sheer bad manners in public life had been simply unthinkable.

The events outside the Assembly that year showed clearly that Paisley was now directly targeting the Protestant middle ground as well as the Unionist Party itself. Ironically, it also provided an opportunity for the crusading editor of the *Belfast Telegraph* to make one of the most important speeches of his life.

It was an honour for John E. Sayers to be invited to address the Presbyterian General Assembly, which at that time was one of the 'holiest of holies' in Ulster's religious life. I cannot think of any other newspaper editor who was given this honour since then, and I have worked for all seven *Telegraph* editors who succeeded him in the past fifty-six years.

This honour was also a reflection on Sayers's high standing in Northern Irish society. In 1963 Queen's University awarded him an honorary doctorate of literature, which he regarded as one of the greatest accolades of his career. He was a regular broadcaster on local BBC Radio. In his prime time slots he urged people on all sides to work for the best for everyone in Northern Ireland. He had very close connections with key figures like Terence O'Neill and had made friendly contact with the Catholic primate, Cardinal William Conway. He had gone out of his way to broaden his Catholic contacts, and had spoken – for example – at the annual dinners of St Malachy's Old Boys and the Belfast Christian Brothers Past Pupils' Union. St Malachy's and Belfast Christian Brothers were among the most important Catholic grammar schools in the city.

Without doubt, his invitation to speak to the General Assembly was well deserved. His speech could not have come at a more dramatic time – the evening following Paisley's intervention. The difference between the visionary and the reactionary could not have been more obvious.

Taking as his theme the 'Communication of the Christian Faith through the Printed Word', Sayers said, 'I have to look towards all the people of Northern Ireland; observe all the factors by which their lives are ruled. Again and again I have to conclude that there is much in our society that is wrong and that only the spirit of God can really put right.

'The wrongs are not only in moral weakness and antagonisms in individuals. They exist in the system, in the divisions and inherited prejudices and practices that we must confess are at variance with God's law. As such they call for the Churches to condemn them and to lead the way towards their correction. In the province, as it is today, it is impossible for the Churches *not* to be aware of conflicts that are harmful to every one of us.'

Sayers warned prophetically that 'it is only by recognising the problems of separation and hostility and the Christian responsibility for solving them, that we can establish that the Churches still have a mission … *The* Church is … a body of Christian citizens with a commission to bring about all the reforms that may be necessary.

'This can only mean a quickening of the Christian conscience. If we do not have that, I am afraid that in the changes which are forcing themselves on Northern Ireland today, the Churches may find themselves excluded … If there is to be a fairer and happier society, a society based on the best foundations, it can only be created by us and of God.'

He continued, 'I am not a dreamer. I know full well that we are facing a tangle of history and geography and emotions deep-writ on human hearts that has made good men despair before now. But I believe that we are called today on every political and religious ground, to try again, and that this time we have a real hope of making this island at peace with itself.'[14]

This speech was written for a church audience, but it was a remarkable speech by any standard, and it confirmed that Sayers's mission to help create a better society came from a deep Christian commitment as a practising Methodist. This was underlined by his close friend the Reverend Dr Eric Gallagher, a Methodist Church President, who underlined Sayers's 'sheer Christian integrity'. Here was a crusading editor who believed that healing deep divisions was a Christian imperative, not just a political and social objective that made good sense.

Jack Sayers's practice of Methodism was regarded by many of us as something that we ought never to forget when reporting for the *Belfast Telegraph*. It was always high on the list of our news editors' priorities, whatever else was taking place in the world beyond the Methodist Church, and to me and my fellow journalists it was just one of our editor's little quirks.

I was not aware then of Jack's deep faith, which he did not wear on his sleeve, but with hindsight I realise that it was at the core of his life. It is only now, some sixty years later, that I have begun to wonder if this was also related to his near-death experience when his ship was sunk by a German U-boat in the cold Atlantic, and his miraculous escape with his life when hundreds of his naval colleagues perished.

Perhaps Sayers felt that his life had been spared for a reason. What better way to fulfil that destiny than to serve in Churchill's Map Room to help defeat Hitler's Germany, and later to try to heal the ancient divisions in Northern Ireland? The man who appointed me to my first job in journalism was a much bigger person than I could have imagined way back in 1964.

The contrast between the words and actions of Sayers and Paisley only one evening apart in June 1966 confirmed that a deep struggle was indeed taking place for the soul of Northern Ireland. This was recognised by many people. Only a month after his General Assembly speech, Sayers received a letter from Mr Edmund Gordon, the headmaster of a leading grammar school in County Antrim.

He wrote, 'I think it is important for some of us who believe in the things you stand for to make it clear how much we admire the courage and firmness and clarity and moderation which you have shown in dealing with the present problems, and particularly that of Paisleyism.

'Over the past couple of years, one has come to regard you and the *Telegraph* as the spearhead against racism and bigotry, and the ugly anachronisms that befoul Ulster life. Without you, indeed, one would at times have almost given up hope, because there was no other voice to speak [the] truth and not be afraid.'[15]

Sayers was clearly making a wide impact, but so too was Paisley, by his use of the media, and the creation of his own *Protestant Telegraph* newspaper in opposition to the *Belfast Telegraph*. This was almost a backhanded compliment to Jack Sayers and his colleagues.

One particular editorial in the *Protestant Telegraph* underlined Paisley's fury at Sayers: '… Foremost in the fray is that fivepenny falsehood known as the *Belfast Telegraph*. For sheer lying and dishonesty, this fifth-rate excuse for a newspaper deserves special condemnation.

'This alleged newspaper once commanded respect. The advent of Sayers and Wallace [the deputy editor] has altered that. Nevertheless this smear sheet has accomplished its evil work. Having for years presented Dr Paisley as a bigot, lawbreaker, hatemonger and vicious extremist, it has convinced certain people that this rubbish is true.

'The *Belfast Telegraph* has set Dr Paisley up as a target for every evil-intentioned thug. If every reader of the *Protestant Telegraph* determined not to buy the *Belfast Telegraph* and influenced his friends to do likewise, the scribbling serpents of Royal Avenue would have their fangs drawn.'[16]

By the end of 1966 the battle for the soul of Ulster was still at its height, and the outcome was by no means certain. As time went on there were signs that O'Neill was having trouble in his own party from those who thought that he was moving too fast in trying to drag Unionism and its more traditional supporters out of the past.

He also failed to convince many Catholics that he was moving fast enough and that he was delivering on some of his key promises for equality on jobs, housing and other dimensions of a truly shared society. This was also a major factor in the rapid growth of the civil rights movement, with supporters taking to the streets and in many cases attracting hostile receptions from Loyalists. The outlook remained uncertain, but within a short time the storm would engulf everything.

7

The Storm Breaks

'The difficulty lies, not in the new ideas, but in escaping the old ones'

John Maynard Keynes, British economist (1883–1946)

These words from Keynes summarise precisely the challenge facing the people of Northern Ireland some five decades after the partition of the island of Ireland. The challenge was either to stride bravely towards a better future, or to keep looking back, do nothing and remain trapped in sectarianism and violence while the wider world went on its own way.

Despite Terence O'Neill's attempts to bring Northern Ireland into a greater realisation of the need for change, he faced increasing opposition from his own side and disillusion from the Nationalist community at the slow pace of change. Sadly, within an all too short period the situation spiralled out of control and Northern Ireland began to make the wrong headlines nationally and internationally. For the next few decades those headlines kept coming again and again.

Discrimination against Catholics in housing and employment and in other areas galvanised the burgeoning civil rights campaign. This was backed by some Unionists as well as Nationalists, but the more hard-line Loyalists and Unionists worked to thwart it at every turn, leading to physical clashes. The Royal

Ulster Constabulary, in its role of keeping the peace, was brought further into the conflict.

Matters began to come to a head in June 1968 when Austin Currie, my old Queen's University classmate who had won a seat as a Nationalist Stormont MP, squatted in an empty house in Caledon, near the border, to illustrate the discrimination against Catholics in the allocation of public housing. The house had been earmarked by the local council for a young Protestant woman who, according to a subsequent report by the Cameron Commission, could not be regarded 'as a priority tenant'. Austin Currie's action received widespread publicity.

In October that year a civil rights march through Londonderry had been banned by the government, but when it went ahead anyway, the marchers were batoned by the police in full view of the television cameras. One of the marchers was the prominent Nationalist Westminster MP, Gerry Fitt, who knew well that one picture was worth a thousand stories, and his bloodied brow made many headlines in the local, national and international media.

Historian Jonathan Bardon summarised the crisis succinctly in his definitive history of Ulster: 'At a stroke the television coverage of events of 5 October 1968 destabilised Northern Ireland, and as the sectarian dragon was fully re-awakened, the region was plunged into a near-revolutionary crisis, characterised by bitter intercommunal conflict and protracted violence and destruction.'[17]

In response Terence O'Neill announced reforms that gave the civil rights protesters much of what they had demanded. It seemed to some Unionists, including Jack Sayers, that this might be enough to turn the tide. In fact, Sayers sent me on a fact-finding mission around Northern Ireland to gauge grass-roots opinion. It was not the equivalent of an opinion poll, but a reporter with mind and ears open can learn a lot by listening to voters talking about their frustrations as well as their aspirations.

After a week or so on the road I had heard enough to make me release that the job of re-establishing social stability would be much more difficult than moderate Unionists and others might realise.

Jack Sayers ran my articles under the headline 'The 50 Days Revolution'. None of us realised at the time that this 'revolution' would lead to decades of the most horrific violence and unrest. With hindsight, it seems that Sayers was greatly over-optimistic, and within a few weeks of the Derry confrontation, the seriousness of the situation was underlined by O'Neill's keynote address on television on 9 December, which became known as the 'Crossroads speech'.

He began, 'Ulster stands at the crossroads. For more than five years now I have tried to heal some of the deep divisions in our community. I did so because I could not see how an Ulster divided against itself could hope to stand. I made it clear that a Northern Ireland based upon the interests of any one section rather than upon the interests of all could have no long-term future.'

He pointedly asked his listeners, 'What kind of Ulster do you want?' and said '... the choice is yours. If it is your decision that we should live up to the words "Ulster is British", which is part of our creed, then my services will be at your disposal to do what I can.'

He warned, however, that '... if you should want a separate, inward-looking, selfish and divided Ulster then you must seek for others to lead you along that road, for I cannot and will not do it. Please weigh well all that is at stake, and make your voice heard in whatever way you think best, so that we may know the views not of the few but of the many.

'For this is truly a time of decision, and in your silence all that we have built up could be lost.

... I pray that you will reflect carefully and decide wisely. And I ask all our Christian people, whatever their denomination, to attend their places of worship on Sunday next to pray for the peace and harmony of our country.'[18]

It was one of the best speeches of O'Neill's premiership, and apparently he wrote it with the help of two key civil service advisers, Kenneth Bloomfield and Jim Malley. It was generally well-received, even though O'Neill's political enemies in his own party were not impressed. Only time would tell if it would steer the province away from violence and political deadlock.

Jack Sayers warmly embraced the sentiments of the speech, and printed 'I Back O'Neill' coupons in the *Belfast Telegraph*. Within a short time O'Neill received some 150,000 messages of support. Significantly, however, it was noted in many quarters that in backing O'Neill so comprehensively, Sayers could be accused of a lack of political detachment in his paper's coverage of the political battles that were swirling all around. There was no doubt that this former Royal Navy officer had nailed his colours firmly to the mast.

O'Neill ended the year in a seemingly better position, but he could not rely on the support of his party, despite assurances of loyalty from those who were secretly plotting against him. In a desperate attempt to gauge how much support he had across the country, O'Neill called a general election for 24 February 1969. In the event he did better than many expected, with twenty-seven pro-O'Neill candidates returned, compared to ten who were anti-O'Neill. It was worrying, however, that Paisley obtained only 1,414 fewer votes than the PM in O'Neill's Bannside constituency, which was a humiliation.

The opposition to O'Neill was relentless from those who believed that any significant concessions to the Nationalist minority would lead inevitably to a united Ireland. However, it is also important to stress that many Nationalists did not recognise Northern Ireland's constitution and still supported a united Ireland, while too few Catholics were prepared to join the police force, one of the main pillars of society. Because of this attitude many Unionists felt that they were right to be wary of any moves to make concessions to the Catholic and Nationalist population.

Despite his best efforts, O'Neill knew that he had lost the argument, and on 29 April he resigned, largely forced out by his colleagues. His departure was a landmark in the history of Northern Ireland, and the opportunity for a peaceful, progressive and tolerant province fit for the twentieth century and beyond would be lost for a distressingly long time.

Jack Sayers also knew that the game was up, and he must have been deeply depressed, even though he put on a brave face in a letter to a long-term confidant shortly before O'Neill resigned. He said, 'I've been editing the paper since 1953, so I've had a fair run and no regrets. It was a satisfaction to get back for the election and to lend the PM a hand. We got very wedded to him – partly for want of anyone better – and it is well that Martin [Wallace] should start to take a more independent view. I don't doubt that his turn as editor will come.'[19]

Sayers was wrong about Martin Wallace, his deputy, who never became editor of the *Belfast Telegraph*. Instead the post went to Eugene Wason, an experienced Scot who had edited a paper in Rhodesia and had stood up bravely against the regime of Ian Smith. Wason was totally different from Sayers – more approachable, more populist in his coverage of events, and, most importantly, an outsider.

Like many other outsiders he could never understand why so many Protestants and Catholics went to church every Sunday to worship the same God, and yet they were unable to vote for politicians who would rule their own country with tolerance and mutual understanding. In other words they prayed for peace, but repeatedly voted for political conflict, unwittingly or not. I often wondered what God made of it all. Eugene Wason used to shake his head sorrowfully and say, 'As for me, I find my God on the golf course on Sunday mornings.'

I was also disappointed by the slow progress towards better community relations, particularly as I had experienced the rapport between Protestants and Catholics in my native village of Bessbrook, even though they worshipped in different churches each Sunday. This was clearly not happening across Northern Ireland. Too many people were keeping the faith within their respective denominations, but not stepping outside to reach across the boundaries. Politically they kept faith with their political parties, with very few people voting across the divides. Collectively they were all keeping the faith, but they were also failing miserably to make Northern Ireland a better place for people from all faith backgrounds and none.

Back in the *Belfast Telegraph* I had more to think and write about than politics. When Jack Sayers appointed me as a leader writer I asked him for a rise, but he said, 'Good God, man, think of the honour', and he meant it. A pay rise did come but it was not enough, so I decided to approach his successor, Eugene Wason, who had a great gift for dealing with his staff. One afternoon when I asked him for a pay rise, Eugene sat in his big chair in his office, with his thumbs plucking his red braces, beaming at me across the table. He said, 'Alf, on your best days you write like an angel and I would love to give you the increase in salary you need, and even more than that, but I don't have the money to do so.' He was one of the few bosses I worked for who could give you a 'No' for an answer, but leave you feeling better!

Eugene maintained the *Telegraph*'s cross-community policy, and his successor, Roy Lilley, whom he groomed for the job, had also been one of Sayers's stalwarts, and continued the policy through the worst years of the Troubles. Roy also became a mentor of mine and in later years we were as close as brothers. Some time before he died he asked me to speak at his funeral, and it was one of the most difficult addresses of my life. I still miss him as a friend and colleague.

Looking back on the Sayers years at the *Telegraph*, they were much more pivotal than I realised at the time. The period from roughly 1964 to 1968 was the last opportunity to snatch peace from the jaws of impending inter-community violence. In 1968 Jack Sayers was nominated by *Hibernia* in Dublin as 'Ireland's most courageous editor', but by that time he was a spent man in ill health, and his political vision had been darkened and then obliterated by subsequent events. Deep down he must have been heartbroken, but he was a true Brit with the stiff upper lip discipline of his naval training, and he said nothing to us in the newspaper, apart, no doubt, from some private conversations with people in his inner circle.

Jack retired on 17 March 1969 and died some five months later on 30 August, just a fortnight or so after the fierce clashes between the police and rioters in Derry which became known as 'The Battle of the Bogside'. Sayers's worst fears were realised then, just shortly before he took his last breaths, but his death spared him the many years of most awful violence that was to come.

Terence O'Neill went to live in England after he retired, and I recall covering for the *Belfast Telegraph* the story of the public auction of his house shortly before he left. He seemed to me to be a very sad man, and for very good reasons. In his autobiography, published in 1972, he recalled, 'as the Unionist Party members were unwilling to change I was largely, though not entirely, reduced to improving relations between Catholics and Protestants in Northern Ireland and also relations between Northern Ireland and Southern Ireland … So now as I finally bring these memoirs to a close I wonder what the future will bring. The recent past has been so terrible that I find it hard to forecast anything remotely reassuring.

'The sad thing is that there are so many people on both sides of the great religious divide who fail to appreciate that but for the presence of the British Army, a civil war would have been raging for the last two or three years. One of these days, hatreds and suspicions in Ireland will have to be brought to an end. Let us hope that it will be sooner rather than later.'[20]

There was a grim and bitter irony that the year 1972, when O'Neill's memoirs were published, was the worst of the entire Troubles, a year in which 470 people died, including 322 civilians and 148 members of the security forces. This was only three years after O'Neill resigned and Jack Sayers died. The baleful future that they had feared and had tried to prevent, had arrived with a vengeance.

The period from 1964 to 1968 has perhaps been overlooked or underestimated by some commentators as a last window for peace before the deluge of violence swept across the province. In re-reading the details of those years, and recalling my first-hand experience as a young reporter for the *Belfast Telegraph* at that time, I have been filled by a deep sadness for what might have been. When the Unionists rejected O'Neill and his progressive ideas, they took a path where, over the decades, they made the wrong decisions in most of the big challenges, and doomed themselves to lose influence and power on an island and in a province that was to change beyond their comprehension politically.

Perhaps O'Neill started his bridge-building too late, and certainly he was remiss in not building a stronger power-base among his own colleagues. Jack Sayers may have been too optimistic, at times naive, about the reality of bridge-building, and in the developing television age he may have overestimated the power of the *Belfast Telegraph* to influence public opinion strongly enough to make a permanent change in the political landscape of Northern Ireland. The work that both men tried to do should have started long before either reached such high office, but the cold apartheid period between the Irish Republic and Northern Ireland since Partition made the necessary bridge-building impossible.

There was also the considerable and negative influence of the Reverend Ian Paisley in thwarting liberal Unionism and bridge-building at every turn. These were the days long before the establishment of the Provisional IRA, who later entered into the fray with their own vicious agenda, which made compromise almost impossible.

Thus, many people regard Paisley as one of the men most responsible for the outbreak of the Troubles. There is considerable truth in this. At a time when liberal Unionists and people like O'Neill and Sayers were trying to build a better Ulster, Paisley and his followers were looking to the past of 'No Surrender' and 'Not An Inch'. Paisley's eloquence and shrewd political manipulation constantly stoked the fears of those who felt that bridge-building meant a surrender to the enemies of Ulster.

It is interesting to note that Sayers and O'Neill, both ex-Service veterans, had considerable experience of the Second World War – Sayers having been shipwrecked in the Atlantic and having worked in Churchill's Map Room, and O'Neill having served as an officer with the 6th Guards Tank Brigade. Two of his brothers died in the war. Perhaps it is no coincidence that my friend the Reverend Ray Davey, the former Presbyterian Dean of Residence at Queen's University, who had also served in the war, also saw the urgent need to make peace at home. Perhaps all three men were too far ahead of their time.

It is sad that Sayers and O'Neill have been long forgotten in the ever-changing kaleidoscope of Northern Ireland politics, and the feeling is that somehow they failed. It could also be argued that their courageous campaign against the odds also sowed some of the seeds of community bridge-building and the rejection of violence that underpinned the historical Good Friday Agreement of 1998. In those intervening years, many thousands of people from both communities in Northern Ireland and further afield paid a terrible price for the mistakes of those who had rejected the path of peace some thirty years earlier. In 1968 Terence O'Neill and, by implication, Jack Sayers, had asked the people, 'What kind of Ulster do you want?'

Sadly, they soon got their answer, as Northern Ireland sank into decades of unrest and became a byword for violence. At times it was a political basket-case and often seemed ungovernable. That was not the kind of Ulster that I, or many others like me, wanted, but we had to grit our teeth and try to do the best we could in the worst of times.

8

The Dogs of War

When people talk about the 'Troubles' in Northern Ireland, that Irish euphemism for death, suffering, misunderstanding, bitterness, cruelty and immense personal tragedy, it seems far away, even though I lived and worked as a journalist through it all.

Recently I watched a part of the BBC's acclaimed television series *Once Upon A Time in Northern Ireland*, and I was reminded of the graphic details of the period during the Hunger Strike from 1980–81.

My reaction was, 'How on earth did I and others live through all of this violence, which was unfolding before our very eyes every day?' Few people want to talk about the past, with all its horrors, and when I do so to a group, or to individuals (especially younger people), I feel like a veteran war correspondent. I now understand why my grandfather Tommy McCreary and my uncle Denzil Jones were so reluctant to talk about their wars at the Somme and in Burma respectively.

This is partly because it is difficult to convey to people the fear of those times, when each day could be your last, and also the noises and smells of violence and of the sulphur in the air. There is also the complication of trying to give shocking statistics a human dimension. Recently I read that at the Battle of Borodino, some sixty miles west of Moscow, on 7 September 1812, the French and Russian armies lost some 75,000 men between them in a pitched battle that went on from 6.00 am until nightfall. A few days ago I heard a television reporter give an estimate that some

500,000 soldiers have died since the beginning of the war between Ukraine and Russia, which was started by the monstrous Putin. How do you begin to grasp that each of these statistics covers the story of a person who was born, grew up, had a family, perhaps had a dream, and had their life cut short, often with little or no recognition, apart from what was left of their friends and families.

The statistics for Northern Ireland show that from the start of the Troubles in 1969 until the signing of the Good Friday Agreement in 1998, a total of 3,289 people died, including 2,332 civilians. During this period there were 35,669 shootings, 10,142 explosions, 5,104 devices defused, 20,568 armed robberies and over £29 million stolen.[21]

These figures for such a small province and its relatively small population of 1.5 million are shocking, and difficult to absorb in the round. However, when you begin to realise that each of these events involved human beings, your shock and sense of tragedy begins to deepen.

It is a sad irony that people on all sides and the politicians they elected who could not find a path to peace, did share one grotesque fate. By failing to agree, they shared the same suffering and loss of loved ones, and they also shared the dangers of daily life in a place convulsed by violence and deadlock for more than three decades.

From 1968 until late 1984, when I left full-time employment in the *Belfast Telegraph*, I reported at first hand on a large number of incidents during the Troubles, and I interviewed scores of victims on both sides of the religious and political divides. From 1985, in my new job as Head of Information at Queen's, I was able to keep in touch with the latest developments, partly as the university itself made headlines that were embarrassing to the institution, in terms of equal opportunities in employment and also in dropping the British national anthem at its graduation ceremonies, which enraged loyalists and also disappointed rank-and-file Unionists. They felt that a university that had been named after Queen Victoria in 1845 should also be allowed to play the national anthem at its graduation ceremonies.

During my time at Queen's I also wrote articles for a wide range of publications, including the *Irish Times*, the *Christian Science Monitor* in Boston, *Time* magazine and the *London Evening Standard*. However, in my years of reporting directly for the *Belfast Telegraph* and other news sources, I was torn between dealing with what had become a national and international story, and reporting on the victims, who were my own people in Northern Ireland.

It was great rubbing shoulders with the visiting big boys, such as the reporters from *Time* and *Newsweek*, the *Sunday Times*, the *Guardian* and other top publications, who came to Northern Ireland to cover some of the major stories. However, when the star reporters flew out again, the aftermath of the violence they had covered remained all too real for me and my colleagues, and the people around us.

One of the first big local stories occurred on Saturday 4 March 1972, when a bomb planted by the Provisional IRA exploded without warning in the crowded Abercorn Restaurant in the middle of Belfast. The blast killed two young women and injured seventy other people, some of them very severely. I heard the boom several miles away, but the next day I flew out early with a group of journalists on a visit to Gibraltar and Morocco.

It was only much later that I learned in detail about the horrific aftermath of the Abercorn bomb. This was during my research for a book called *Survivors*, which was one of the first to give a graphic account of the suffering during the Troubles. My aim was to show people that in hospitals there was no 'Protestant' or 'Catholic' blood, and that the suffering was experienced by people from all backgrounds. It now seems a noble if rather naive motive, especially as the situation worsened later on, and some hospital wards were guarded by the security forces because the patients inside were injured paramilitaries

The Royal Victoria Hospital was officially unhelpful about helping me to write their story, of which they had every right to be proud, but I was given great unofficial assistance by the hospital consultants and other staff. Within a couple of years I was able to finish my book, which by that stage covered the work of several of the main hospitals in Northern Ireland.

One person I remember particularly was Jimmy Hughes, who had stepped in to the Abercorn Restaurant on that fateful Saturday afternoon to have a snack. He was caught up in the blast, and his legs were badly injured. When I talked to him while doing research for the book, I realised that he was a 'born again' Christian and a Sunday school teacher, and that his faith had given him great strength in such dire circumstances. He told me was it was like to be told by the doctors that he had lost his limbs. That was the kind of story that was not reported in detail by the media, but it gave me a disturbing idea of the reality of violence. I also talked to two sisters, Rosaleen and Jennifer McNern, who also lost limbs, and faced their future with inspiring courage.

Jimmy Hughes was engaged to be married to Florrie when the Abercorn explosion took place. Undaunted, they were married over two years later in the Welcome Evangelical Church in Cambrai Street, Belfast, before a large congregation of family, friends and well-wishers. Jimmy sat in a chair during the wedding ceremony, but with great determination he walked proudly down the aisle beside Florrie using two sticks. They spent their honeymoon in Blackpool and later set up home in a modern bungalow north of Belfast.

Florrie said to me, 'The explosion came as a real blow, but like Jimmy I am a Christian, and I believe that the Lord wanted us to be together. I always knew we were right for one another. You just had to admire Jimmy's fight to recover. It was a long hard struggle.' Jimmy told me, 'When you come so close to death, you see just how great life is. I am just glad to be alive, and my disabilities don't get me down. I only feel sorry for the people who put me in this condition. They just don't know how great life can be.'

A few years after their marriage I visited Jimmy and Florrie at their home, when I was arranging to have their wedding picture placed on the cover of my book *Survivors*. When I entered Jimmy's living-room he was sitting on the floor with his children, but without wearing his artificial limbs. He asked me cheerfully, 'How are things, Alfie?' In reply I told him about my problems, about the late deadlines I had to face, about the traffic difficulties in getting to his house, and about my worries in general. Then I asked him, 'How are you, Jimmy?' He stunned me with his reply. 'Alfie, I can't complain.' I felt humbled and ashamed. I have remembered that story for many years, and when I am in a complaining mood I think of Jimmy, and of the innocent people injured in the Troubles, and I say to myself, 'Catch yourself on.'

I also learned from the Troubles that there were many others who were scarred in unexpected ways. During an interview for my profile radio programme on BBC Northern Ireland, I talked to a charming and urbane surgeon called Willoughby Wilson, who had operated on many of the victims of violence. He told me how he had immediately walked off his golf course one Saturday when he heard a large bomb explode miles away in Belfast. He knew that he would be needed in the Royal Victoria Hospital, and shortly after he arrived there he had to tell a young man that two of his children had been killed in the blast. Willoughby said, 'When he heard that he kneeled down and banged his head off the floor so many times that he started to bleed. He was beside himself with grief.'

As Willoughby Wilson told me this he began to break down at the memory and started to cry. We had to take a break in the interview which, luckily, was being recorded for a later transmission. However, I realised that this distinguished surgeon, who had so often put on a brave face during the worst of times, had become a victim of violence himself, and that he also was a casualty of the war.

Another doctor I remember was William Rutherford, the consultant in charge of A&E at the Royal Victoria Hospital when the Troubles started. I knew him well. He was a devout Christian who had served for several years as a medical missionary in India. William was slow of speech and you never quite knew what was coming out of his mouth, but he was a man of great charm and integrity, and had an air of calm and commitment when dealing with the victims of violence who were brought to him in their distress. I have no doubt that this arose from his strong inner faith, which sustained him through very difficult times. William was one of the best examples I ever met of a person literally 'keeping the faith'.

The violence affected many different people in different ways, even if their victimhood was self-inflicted. I interviewed one bright young Ulster businessman who decided after much thought that the best way to settle the Northern Ireland problem was to join the Provisional IRA. I found this attitude incredible in such an intelligent man, but his story was fascinating.

On his first mission with the Provisionals he was caught up in a gun battle with the security forces and was arrested. He was convicted of terrorist offences, and given a long prison sentence. His membership of the IRA was so secret that even his wife did not know about it until he was caught.

While in prison he remained bitter, and associated himself with other Republican paramilitaries. However, one day he found out about a bible class that had been formed in the prison, and he went along 'as a joke', but he became so impressed with the teaching that he eventually attended the meetings regularly and began to pray and to read the Bible for himself. He was supported by others and he eventually became a Christian. His life changed for the better, and he bitterly regretted causing so much unnecessary suffering to his wife and family, and also to himself.

Since that interview we have lost touch, but I sincerely hope that he has stayed on the right path. There are many people who sneer at such stories of Christian conversion and claim cynically that these are merely examples of 'I got found out and I found God'. I do not share that view. If a conversion to Christianity changes a person's life in a good way, who am I to criticise him or her, or to judge whether the conversion is real or not? I believe that God often works in a mysterious way, and that the influence of the Holy Spirit can be all-powerful in the most unlikely situations.

However, I am not suggesting that it is only people of Christian faith who can rebuild their lives. When I was writing a book called *Tried By Fire*, about the victims of violence, I spoke at length to Jane Ewart-Biggs the widow of British Ambassador to Ireland Christopher Ewart-Biggs, who was murdered by the Provisional IRA in Dublin on 21 July 1976. He was fifty-four. He died when his armoured Jaguar car was bombed by a landmine at Sandymount on its way to the British Embassy in Dublin. He had had a distinguished war record, had joined the Foreign Service, and became associated with MI6.

Jane and Christopher had three young children. She later became a life peer in the House of Lords, established the Christopher Ewart-Biggs Memorial Prize for Literature, and campaigned for better Anglo-Irish relations. When I talked to her for the book she told me, 'I wanted to bring something sane out of this act of insanity, so it seemed the right thing to stay in Dublin and to make a bond with Ireland against the enemy of reason and sanity.

'I believe in all the Christian ethics, even though I am an agnostic. I believe in the Christian rules that govern the community. I don't go to church, but I can believe in other people's beliefs. Very often I do things in churches.

'In Westminster Cathedral they had a great ecumenical service on St Patrick's Day when they wanted people to pause and reflect on Northern Ireland. I took a leading part in that, not on a religious theme, but one based on humanity. For me the individual concerned is the positive force. Hatred only hates itself, and Ireland is an example of what hatred has done.

'Reconstruction can be made through religious or human resources. I can see how someone can reconstruct something on religious grounds, prayer and that kind of thing, it's a sort of catalyst. But if you don't have that, it has to be built on faith in human beings, in human terms, but the faith has to be great. People who are religious do sometimes tend to remain within themselves because they get comfort. My way of getting comfort is outside myself.'[22]

I was very impressed by Jane's honesty, courage and vision, and our meeting reminded me of the importance of keeping an open mind when writing about matters of faith. During the Troubles I had to interview far too many suffering people from every religious background and from none. Some people were helped by their faith, others seemed not to have a faith, but there were also those who had a strong belief in the innate goodness of human beings, and the importance of hope.

Jane Ewart-Biggs's words on hope were uttered a long time ago but they are still relevant today and to people from all backgrounds. She said, 'My faith is that good triumphs, though my own experience has not worked out that way very much. I do need to have that faith, and therefore I build my hope on what I know is good in Northern Ireland. One can have faith that the positive ingredients will win. If they are given time.'[23]

One of the biggest stories of all was the murder of Lord Mountbatten of Burma on the sunny August bank holiday in 1979 when a Provisional IRA bomb destroyed the small boat in which he and members of his family were lobster-fishing in Donegal Bay. Several years later I had a long interview with his daughter, Countess Mountbatten, whose twin son Nicholas died in the blast, along with a local boy, Paul Maxwell. Her mother-in-law, Lady Brabourne, died the next day. Countess Mountbatten and her husband Lord Brabourne were badly injured in the explosion but they recovered after a sustained and painful period of recuperation.

During the long interview in her apartment in London she spoke to me frankly and movingly. She said, 'I have not at any time felt anti-Irish, not in any way. In the Sligo hospital they were trying to put us together again, and they felt terrible about what had happened. When we were transferred to a hospital in England, the Irish nurses told me that they felt so ashamed. We tried to reassure them that we loved Ireland and that the people who had done this could not really be regarded as representatives of their country.

'I believe strongly in hope. If you lose hope you lose all desire to live. What brought me through was the realisation that I was still alive, and that I had better get on with it, and that the family still needed me, and that I could not go around moping miserably, because it wasn't fair to them.'[24]

As she talked and showed me the family photographs her eyes frequently welled up with tears. I was reminded yet again that human suffering knows no bounds, whether it is in Knightsbridge in London, the Bogside in Derry or in a terraced house in east Belfast.

Events moved on in the years after I spoke at great length to these remarkable women.

Jane Ewart-Biggs died aged sixty-two, some six years before the signing of the Good Friday Agreement which, despite its flaws, ended the killing and maiming that had been taking place on an almost industrial scale. Countess Mountbatten died in 2017, aged ninety-three, but she lived long enough to see that the Good Friday Agreement had made a vast improvement in the situation in Northern Ireland, even if the sporadic violence continued, as did the political deadlock.

I am filled with respect for both women for their lack of bitterness at the deaths of their loved ones through terrorism, and their hopes for better relations between Britain and Ireland – the island that had caused them such grief – and within Northern Ireland itself. They were women of their time but they were, and are, also timeless. Their contributions to reconciliation ought not to be forgotten, just like the efforts of many others who did not make the headlines but whose contributions to greater understanding should never be overlooked.

Reporting the Troubles taught me above all that keeping the faith can be costly and difficult, but without faith in a better future, we have nothing to hope for.

9

More Blood and Tears

On Sunday, 30 January 1972, soldiers from the British Parachute Regiment fired on a large crowd of civilians who were on a protest march in Londonderry organised by the Northern Ireland Civil Rights Association. Thirteen marchers died, and another civilian died from injuries a few months later. Other people were injured, some of them badly.

There had been foreboding in the days and hours leading up to the march, but no one had expected a mass killing. It created uproar and outrage, as well as immense grief and suffering. It also proved to be a turning point in the Troubles, because the Northern Ireland authorities had lost any grip they had had on the declining situation. It led to the suspension of the Stormont administration, and the imposition of direct rule from Westminster.

The Bloody Sunday massacre also led to a deterioration of relations between London and Dublin, where the British Embassy building was burned down by protesters. Bloody Sunday also proved to be a major boost to recruitment for the Provisional IRA, and the bitterness created by this appalling mass murder festered for decades, until British Prime Minister David Cameron formally apologised on 15 June 2010 for the killings, which he described as 'unjustified' and 'unjustifiable'. The Saville Report, published on the same day after twelve years of detailed investigation, stated that the paratroopers had 'lost control' and that soldiers had 'lied' to hide their acts.

This contrasted sharply with the conclusions of the earlier Widgery Tribunal of April 1972, which had largely exonerated the soldiers and was widely regarded as a whitewash. The aftermath of Bloody Sunday still remains controversial, with the relatives of the victims and others still demanding the prosecution of those responsible for the killings.

On the day after the shootings I was sent post-haste to Derry by Eugene Wason to report on the immediate aftermath of the violence and to cover the funerals, which were to take place two days later. At that point in my career I had not been asked to report on such a massive story, and I did not know what to expect. There was no stereotype to follow. I had only my notebook and pen, and the hope that I could locate public phones quickly when I needed them urgently. My news editor had booked me a room in the Broomhill Hotel in Derry, but apart from that I felt that I was on my own. I had to rely on my wits and common sense in reporting a story that had to be carefully balanced for a huge readership of my paper which, in those days of surging print journalism, sold over 200,000 copies daily on both sides of the political and religious divide.

I was immediately struck by the grim atmosphere of silence and mourning in the city. This was reflected by the opening words of my report for the paper – 'Londonderry is a city caught in the cold hand of death. A piercing wind sweeps across Lough Foyle. The weak sun fades in a wintry sky that promises snow. The bitter weather matches the mood of the city.

'Derry is like a prolonged wake. The main streets are empty. The shops are closed. Soldiers with rifles at the ready shelter wearily in the shop doorways, surveying the bleak scene. It is a place where people fend for themselves. The abiding reality, apart from the feelings of death, is the total lack of communication across the divide.

'The story of Derry is the tale of two cities. It is symptomatic of Northern Ireland and of Ireland and its people. Its messages of "We shall overcome" and "Not an inch" are mutually contradictory. Its continuing tragedy is that there seems to be nothing as yet to fill the emptiness. There is too much faith, not enough hope and too little charity.'

As I rewrite these words over fifty years later I am reminded of the atmosphere of despair and hopelessness in which I and my colleagues had to operate, and today I would not change a single word of my report. At the time my main objective was getting a strong enough story to file for the next day's paper, and the opportunity to do so soon presented itself.

The hotel where I was staying in the suburbs of the city was filled with journalists, and while we were all competitors, we were also willing to share opportunities for getting to the heart of the story. So we were relieved to hear that a local doctor and his wife were willing to take several of us down to the Bogside area where the shootings had taken place and to let us hear what the relatives of the dead and injured had to say.

Very quickly I found myself with a gaggle of reporters standing in the Bogside, and listening to the local people. I still clearly remember the advice of the doctor's wife, who said to the young reporter from the *Glasgow Herald*, 'With your Glasgow accent, son, I would keep my mouth shut today if I were you. Some of the paratroopers who were here yesterday had Scottish accents.'

This message conveyed to me the atmosphere of Derry on that dark day. One other detail that disturbed me was the comment of a prominent church-going Protestant in the city. When I asked him to comment on the shootings he said, 'Well, you have to remember that Jesus had to drive the money-changers from the Temple.' Without evidence of what had really happened he was hinting on the day after the killings that in some way the shooting might have been justified. No doubt his thoughts mirrored those of many others throughout the province, and I realised just how deep the divisions were.

One of the major differences in reporting that story over fifty years ago and today was the relative absence of reporters. These were the days before rolling news bulletins filled the airwaves day and night, with every detail analysed infinitely to the point where the shock effect and even the news interest is diluted. My old friend and editor Roy Lilley often said to me, 'The best channel is Sky News, but only for about fifteen minutes until it starts repeating itself.'

In Derry I had to file stories for several editions of the *Belfast Telegraph* each day, but once the paper had gone to press in the late afternoon there were long evenings to fill, and there was more than enough time to reflect on the Derry I had known, and to ask myself what had become of it.

I had first been to Derry in the early 1960s when I was a Queen's University undergraduate attending a residential meeting there with history students from various parts of Ireland. These were the days when Northern Ireland seemed reasonably peaceful, to the point where we thought it a good idea to include a couple of 'party songs' during our revelry in the hotel bar. However, as soon we sang the first notes of 'The Sash', the well-known Orange song, the barman immediately told us to stop. His sense of apprehension that the words might lead to trouble was compelling, and thankfully we had the sense to shut up, even if we thought that perhaps he was being overly fussy. That showed how naive we were. Derry, like Northern Ireland itself, seemed peaceful and politically maturing, but we had no idea of what was lurking beneath the surface.

My first big story from Derry was written in 1968 as part of a request from Jack Sayers to report on 'The Fifty Days' Revolution', just after the upheaval of the Civil Rights march of 5 October when the protesters were batoned by police in full view of the television cameras.

I remember talking to people on both sides as part of my research for this special report, and afterwards I sat reflecting for a long time on a stretch of Derry's famous seventeenth-century walls. Even then I smelt the sulphur in the air. It did not take a genius to release that if the spiral of disorder was not stopped soon there was very serious trouble ahead.

It took only eight months or so for this to become true, with vicious and prolonged disturbances between police and rioters in what came to be called 'The Battle of the Bogside'. This was covered by reporters from all the major news outlets in the UK and Ireland, as well as from Europe and much further afield. I remember Harry Jackson, one of the star *Guardian* reporters, returning wearily from his traumatic experience in Derry and saying to me with a mixture of amazement and despair, 'People on both sides up there still don't want to give in. They want to win.'

After 1969 the situation deteriorated steadily, despite the best efforts of many people to head off the conflict. Perhaps it was no surprise that less than three years later it had got out of hand, with such horrific results for the city and its people, and for any prospect of peace in Northern Ireland.

The day of the funerals dawned dully with a dark cloud of despair hanging over everything and everyone. I made my way early to St Eugene's Roman Catholic Cathedral to pick up more details for my newspaper report before the building filled up and made access to the front difficult. When I arrived, there were few people inside, so I walked up to the altar where the coffins were placed side by side, their name plates reflecting the glimpses of the weak sunlight.

I paused for some time, and then I walked across to the altar and read the name on each coffin. It had been one thing to watch violence and its aftermath on television, which was disturbing enough, but as a young reporter I it felt very difficult to comprehend what I was seeing there in reality. This was death en masse. These people had been alive only a few days ago. Now they were lying in their coffins in the silence and earthly finality of death, while the anguished cries of their families echoed across the pews as the cathedral began to fill up.

I noticed one bereaved relative who was sobbing uncontrollably as she was half-carried into the cathedral by her family. Near her stood Joseph Locke, a well-known and talented Derry professional singer and entertainer, and I thought of how much he had represented the better days of a city that had been brought so low.

In my report I reflected on the deep distress of those innocent people who had lost loved ones, but I was then in my early thirties and was perhaps too young fully to realise what it meant to them. It is only after a long lifetime of witnessing and reporting such trauma in many places, and of experiencing the deaths of my own family members and of close and dear friends that the reality of such loss truly sinks in. I only hope that somehow that funeral service for the Bloody Sunday victims brought some comfort to the bereaved families and that their Christian faith helped them in ways beyond our human understanding.

By the time the funeral service began, the cathedral was packed, with the clergy officiating at the front under the solemn gaze of Cardinal William Conway, who watched the tragic drama slowly unfold before him. Here was the Catholic leader who, only a few years previously, had been in polite correspondence with the Unionist Party leader, Captain Terence O'Neill, when there were hopes of new cross-community shoots of growth emerging after such a long political winter. And now it had come to this.

As the service proceeded I noticed the beautiful music, not surprising in such a musical city, and I listened to a young girl in the gallery choir singing the hymn, 'Through all the changing scenes of life', to the familiar tune of 'Winchester'. I thought to myself, 'That's the same hymn we sing in Protestant churches and the same tune. So what's this all about, why is the Christian message of love and tolerance still falling on so many deaf ears?'

In this mass funeral service the Christian challenge to people from all backgrounds was as urgent as ever. When the service ended, I dashed immediately from the cathedral, found a working phone nearby and I managed to file all my copy just minutes before the deadline for the biggest and final edition of the day, which would be read by people from many different backgrounds across the land. My job was finished and I was exhausted. I felt a mixture of relief and great sadness at such sorrow and loss of life.

That would be the pattern for many other reporters in the years that followed as they brought home the harsh reality of the daily litany of death all across the land. The memory of the Bloody Sunday funerals in Derry lingered long in my mind because it was one of the worst scenes I had ever experienced. Little did I know then that only a few years later I would be called on to report on yet another scene of mass funerals, but this time in a place that had been at the heart of my boyhood, and where I had first heard as a child the central message 'God is love', and the Christian challenge to 'love your neighbour as yourself'. I was to discover yet again that keeping the faith was becoming even more difficult than I had imagined.

10

Murder Most Foul

On a cold early January night in 1976, with the Christmas spirit long gone, my phone rang as I worked in my study at home in Belfast. The *Belfast Telegraph* editor, Roy Lilley, was on the line. He said, 'I have bad news for you. There was a massacre earlier this evening when a large number of men coming back from work were murdered in a roadside ambush in South Armagh. It happened at Kingsmills near your native village of Bessbrook. I want you to go down there first thing tomorrow to report on the aftermath. Find out more and talk to as many locals as you can. I know it will be hard for you, but you are my best staff writer to cover this one. File me as much as you can by early afternoon.'

I was stunned as I put down the phone. Already my mind was racing to grasp the details. How did it happen, why did it happen, how many were killed, did I know any of them? As the evening progressed many of the facts became clearer from the broadcast media. It emerged that a red van carrying twelve workmen from a Glenanne factory had been stopped by unknown gunmen. They were lined up on the road and mown down in cold blood because they were Protestants. The only Catholic had been allowed to escape. The other eleven men had been left for dead, but one of them, Alan Black, had survived and was taken to hospital in nearby Newry.

The attack was thought to have been carried out by the Provisional IRA, or one of its dissident Republican paramilitary offshoots, but no organisation claimed responsibility. The mass murder was allegedly in retaliation for the murder of several Catholics in the local area who were shot by Loyalist paramilitaries in two separate attacks the previous evening. Another young Catholic man died a month later. The Kingsmills atrocity was one of the most shocking and cold-blooded mass murders of the the Troubles. The *Irish Times*, in a striking phrase in its editorial, stated that 'The headless coachman is driving Northern Ireland full tilt down the road to hell.'

I drove to Bessbrook early the next morning to cover one of the most difficult stories of my writing career. I asked myself, 'Where do I start?' I said to myself that I needed to get a grip. One of those who died was in the same class as me at primary school, and many of their grieving relatives were friends of mine. What in God's name was this all about?

As I drove into the village square, and past the house where I had spent my boyhood, I noticed that the Christmas tree was still standing, but without lights, and it was drooping forlornly as if in despair. It matched the mood of the village and its people, and indeed the whole island of Ireland.

Not long after I started talking to people in Bessbrook I met gentle Danny Chapman, who had been a neighbour of mine in The Gardens mixed housing estate. I remembered that Danny walked his racing greyhounds every day, and it was said that when they lost a race, Danny took to his bed for a day to recover, because he was such a sensitive soul.

On that dark day after the vile massacre, Danny had the awful task of identifying two of the victims, his nephews Walter and Reggie Chapman. He told me, 'I cried before I went into the morgue. I expected the worst, and it was the worst. They pulled down the sheets, and there they were, lying dead like dogs, with their teeth showing. It was as awful as that. You can print that.'[25] When he said that, I thought of Walter, who had been not only my school classmate at primary school in Bessbrook, but who had also worked with me delivering post at Christmas to earn a few pounds. Harmless Walter had been lively, and great fun. He had been a human being. Now he was lying brutalised and disfigured, dead like a dog.

After talking to the deeply distressed Danny, I made my way to the home of Jimmy McWhirter, who many years earlier had driven the Bessbrook Mill van which had taken me to the docks in Belfast with my fellow Boy Scouts as we set out for an annual camp in the Isle of Man. It was innocent Jimmy who had driven the van from Kingsmills the night before and he had died in the savage hail of bullets fired by the unknown gunmen.

The wake in Jimmy's house seemed like any other wake, but it was even worse than that because of the prevailing sense of shock and disgust at this murder most foul. People were sitting around, not quite knowing what to say. Someone murmured, 'Thank God he wasn't tortured.' Small consolation indeed. The women busied themselves handing out tea and biscuits. There was nothing else they could do. I shook hands with a dignified Mrs McWhirter who had known me from my early childhood and who was a good friend of my beloved Auntie Jean, who had reared me. There was nothing I could say to Jimmy McWhirter's widow. Our eyes locked silently on each other, and our hand-shake said it all.

As the day wore on, I was conscious of my impending deadline. I went to my mother's house, built on a rock just outside the village, and wrote my report in longhand in her living-room, the exact place where, years earlier, I had experienced the Damascus Road moment of deciding to make my career as a professional writer. It seemed such a tragic turnaround from those earlier days of innocence and hope.

I finished my report with the words 'Maybe after this, or a thousand Bessbrooks, enough people will get the point. Meanwhile as these words on the page crumble in time, and the body of my schoolmate Walter Chapman rots in his grave, the same principle will apply, namely that we will either learn to live together or die together. Thus far we are learning a lot about dying together.'

When I finished writing my report, I phoned it through to the *Telegraph* copy-taker, and then left the village abruptly as the early January darkness began to creep in. My village of Bessbrook, with such happy boyhood memories, had gone for ever. I felt utterly empty.

The next day I was back in Bessbrook for the mass funerals. I had asked Roy Lilley's permission to go there, even though I told him that I would not be writing a line. Roy readily let me go, because he could read me like a book, and he understood. He was a great editor, and a great human being.

The funerals were held in Bessbrook Presbyterian Church where, so many years earlier, I had first heard about God. On the day of the funerals I asked myself, 'Where is God today?' The place was thronged with hundreds of people, and there were television cameras everywhere. The first person I met was my mother Lena. She also understood how I was feeling, and she whispered, 'All those people dead and poor Walter Chapman, your chum from school.'

A little later she said to me matter-of-factly, 'Your father Norman is inside the church. He waited outside and pretended that he was an aide of Ian Paisley. When Paisley arrived he showed him to his seat at the front of the congregation and then sat near him. That's typical of your father.' I knew that he had always been cute and opportunistic, but sadly he was so streetwise that he often outsmarted himself.

Nevertheless my mother's news that he was in the church rocked me back. I had never met him and I had been trying for years to trace him; but that day I determined to track him down. Some months later I did so, but he never admitted to being my father, so there was no happy ending.

Back in the real time of the Bessbrook funerals, I heard the hymns and the several sermons, but in reality I heard nothing. No words or music could make sense on that day. After it was all over I watched the Reverend Paisley standing outside the church, looking over the graveyard. I resented his presence bitterly, as I felt that he was cashing in politically on a mass murder of Protestants, but I also knew that as a party leader he had every right to be there.

Most of all I deeply resented how the terms 'Protestant' and 'Catholic' had been utterly debased on that dreadful night at Kingsmills. I knew that these were tribal labels, often over-used by the media in the need for a short headline, but they were nothing more than that. The brutal reality was that ten men had died and another was badly injured because they were 'Protestants'. The twelfth man had been allowed to escape because he was a 'Catholic'. It was utter sacrilege, and a total debasement of everything that Christianity stood for. And we were paying respects to the dead inside and outside the same church where I had first been told as a child about a good God. That conflict between good and evil highlighted in the funeral services is something that I still remember, and will struggle with for the rest of my life. Keeping the faith can be difficult on occasions, but sometimes it seems almost impossible.

Some months later I returned to Bessbrook to follow up the Kingsmills story. I was writing my book *Survivors*, and it was the first time that this story would feature in a publication about the Troubles. I knew personally the sole survivor, Alan Black, as he was part of the wider Black family of my mother Lena, who was his aunt by marriage. I knew Alan well as a boy in the village, and also his parents, Billy and Bea, who was a particular friend of my mother. They were lovely, decent village people who had been good to me as a boy, and I was very fond of them.

Alan agreed to talk to me in his home in Bessbrook, and he told me his extraordinary story at first hand. It was the first time since the massacre that he had talked in such depth to any journalist. He told me that when the workmen had been lined up on the road, a voice asked 'Who is the Catholic?' The others on each side of Richard Hughes held his hand tightly and whispered, 'Don't move'. They thought that it was the Catholic who was being targeted. Instead it was the Protestants they were after. Once the Catholic man ran off into the darkness, they opened fire on the others and eleven men lay mangled and dead or dying on the cold and damp road.

When the alarm was raised by a passing motorist and his wife, an ambulance sped quickly to the scene from Daisy Hill Hospital in Newry. The paramedics swiftly and systematically assessed the chaotic scene. They spotted six bodies apparently lying dead on the offside of the van, and around the back they nearly fell over other bodies in the darkness.

They quickly realised that Alan Black was still alive, and they set off at speed for the hospital. They were having difficulties with radio signals but they managed to tell the waiting medical staff in code, 'Ten black, one white.' Alan was bordering on unconsciousness but he was perplexed by the crackling radio message of 'ten black'. He felt surely that he was the only Black in the ambulance.

He was rushed into casualty prior to being taken to the operating theatre. By that time the hospital authorities had alerted the only chaplain they could find, and he happened to be a Catholic. As Father Devlin approached Alan he asked tactfully, 'Are you a Catholic?' He did not want to cause offence unknowingly, and he also needed to know whether or not he would be required to administer the Last Rites. Alan had the strength to reply to him, in one of the most poignant understatements imaginable. He said, 'Father, I am not of your flock, but I could do with a prayer anyway.' Immediately Father Devlin took Alan's one uninjured hand and said, 'Keep up your heart, son. You will be all right.' He then said a prayer, and Alan felt a sense of peace.[26]

Later that night Father Devlin conducted a packed service in a large Catholic chapel outside Newry, where the congregation prayed for Alan Black's recovery and for the families and friends of those who had been murdered earlier that evening.

I have long remembered Alan telling me about that moving exchange with Father Devlin before he went into the operating theatre, and for me it symbolised the brutality and the tragedy of the Troubles. In the extremity of life or death there was a shared humanity in being either a Protestant or a Catholic when keeping the faith was a reassurance and a comfort, whatever the theology of that faith happened to be. And for many, but not all, people of no faith, there was concern, sympathy and kindness. These were the kind of intimate exchanges that were overlooked or lost by the general media in the frantic tensions of reporting so much of the Troubles, but they should not be forgotten.

Alan Black had a long and difficult recovery, but against all the odds he survived. He told me about the early days in hospital, which were some of the worst of his recovery. 'I had one bad spell when I would waken about 3.00 am when the effect of the pain-killing injections had worn off. There was the awful pain, and I would think of the Bessbrook boys I would never see again. The nurses seemed to sense that terrible time. I never asked for their help but they just came and sat there. They talked to me until I got back to sleep again. I began to feel that somehow life was worth living again.'[27]

As Alan talked so warmly of those who had helped him, I was reminded yet again of the goodness of so many people who had brought such comfort to others in their time of dire need. It is sometimes tempting to give up hope for a solution to Northern Ireland's problems but I still retain a strong faith in the innate goodness of our people, and the inspiring strength of the human spirit.

After our long interview in Alan's home, I suddenly thought, 'Can we go back to where the massacre took place?' Alan was not sure that his mother would approve, but we went anyhow. As we approached the scene, he noticed a wreath that had been laid on the brow of a slight hill. He said, 'That might be in the wrong place. I remember lying face down in that hollow over there, and the rainwater cooling my cheek when it trickled by me as I lay on the road.' Those words chilled me utterly. I realised that he and I were the only people to stand on the exact spot where the gunmen had opened fire on that horrible night not so long ago. A total of between 150 and 200 rounds had been fired by an alleged twelve gunmen. No fewer than eighteen bullets had riddled Alan Black's body. His survival was a miracle.

Over the years the Kingsmills massacre has been in the headlines often, as attempts have been made to bring the perpetrators to justice. It is extraordinary and deeply disappointing to realise that the authorities have been unable to do so thus far, though a number of people claim to know the identities of some of the alleged gunmen.

Throughout this time there have been many disappointments for the relatives of the Kingsmills victims who despair of any justice and closure as time goes on. I have long admired Alan Black, who has been a major voice in this search for justice. He has always spoken with authenticity and dignity, and he has been a credit to his murdered colleagues and their families.

When he was told of the death of one of the alleged gunmen who took part in the murders at Kingsmills he said, 'He will never be brought to book for slaughtering all those innocent people and for nearly killing me. I feel nothing about his death, but he is with his Maker now and I do feel that people have to answer for their sins.'[28]

Alan said little, but he said everything. He is a fine human being and one of the quiet heroes of the Troubles, unlike those who brutally attacked him in the darkness so long ago, and ended the lives of his colleagues and friends.

Over time the horror and shock of Kingsmills has faded, predictably so, just like the memories of so many other atrocities. Yet for me it remains one of the most searing memories of my lifetime, not only because of the bloodshed and suffering, but because it was so personal in relation to my wider family and earlier background.

I have written about Alan's story at length in other publications, and after the passage of time I thought that I had put it all behind me. Yet, in rereading all the details and now bringing fresh observations about what had happened, I surprisingly found myself reduced to tears. Somehow the old sadness and sense of despair welled up again as I thought of the utter tragedy and loss of life, and it must be the same for thousands of other people on both sides of the divide whose relatives' stories were never highlighted.

Sadly, however, there were just so many more tragedies to try to comprehend. Suffering and sorrow knew no bounds, as events played out in the toxic atmosphere of politics, religion and violence that continually disfigured Northern Ireland. However, there were also those from all backgrounds who were working hard to build bridges of reconciliation and understanding. They were the best of people in the worst of times, and their stories must never be overlooked or taken for granted.

11

The Search for Peace

One of the most impressive Christians I ever met was the Reverend Dr Ray Davey, the Presbyterian chaplain at Queen's University Belfast during my student days there. I was impressed by his graciousness and good humour and also by his muscular Christianity, which had vision and practicality and was grounded in the Gospel and in his experience as a participant in the Second World War.

As a young minister he had volunteered for service as a field secretary with the YMCA. This would almost certainly bring him to the front line of the war, though many of his clerical contemporaries in Northern Ireland chose to follow their vocation in the relative safety of Northern Ireland. That is not to say that they were greater or lesser servants of the Gospel than Ray, but he heard the challenging call and started on a dangerous path, not knowing where it would lead him.

Ray was captured by German troops after the fall of Tobruk during the North African campaign and he spent the next few years incarcerated in a total of six prisoner-of-war camps in Italy and Germany. In his revealing memoirs, *Don't Fence Me In* and the later *War Diaries*, he wrote from a Christian standpoint about the challenges of maintaining morale and hope among the Allied prisoners in times of immense stress and uncertainty. He never forgot those experiences, and he determined to apply the lessons he had learned to the divided society in his native Northern Ireland.

On his return from the war he proved to be a charismatic university pastor to the students who attended meetings at the Presbyterian Centre at Queen's, and out of this grew a vision for a permanent place in Northern Ireland where people of all backgrounds could engage in dialogue and take steps to build bridges across the divides.

A small group of volunteers set about finding a base for the establishment of what came to be known as the Corrymeela Community. They visited other reconciliation centres, including the Iona Community in Scotland, as well as Agape in Italy and Taizé in France. The first meeting of what became the Corrymeela group took place in the Queen's Presbyterian Centre in 1964. Early the following year they heard that a former Holiday Fellowship building situated on the North Coast was up for sale. It had a breathtaking view from its site just outside the town of Ballycastle, with its gorgeous views over the North Channel, along which the Vikings had sailed to pillage the island of Rathlin and where St Columba and his followers had sailed on their journey to Iona, which became a major centre for their Christian mission to Europe.

However there were major snags concerning Corrymeela. The building and grounds needed a great deal of hard work to make the place habitable, and the asking price of £6,500 was a major sum in the mid-sixties. However, there were two encouraging developments, which suggested that this visionary idea might indeed have divine approval. When Ray Davey nervously met the estate agents he was told that they would still honour his bid if the group could raise the money, even though they had received a higher bid. The volunteers gave as much as they could, and there were also generous anonymous donations, including the hefty sum of £2,000 from a single individual. That was a remarkable example of keeping the faith, at a time when there was no guarantee that such a newfangled institution as Corrymeela would actually work. One member recalled that he had lunch or dinner with a large number of high-profile people in

Northern Ireland who were known publicly for their support for reconciliation, but, surprise surprise, none of them actually provided any cash.

After much hard work and preparation, the refurbished building was opened on 30 October 1965 by Pastor Tullio Vinay of Agape, who had travelled from Sicily to share in the simple but impressive ceremony. He told the assembled membership and friends that Corrymeela should be 'a place of encounter and dialogue with everyone, believers and unbelievers', and 'a question mark to the Church everywhere ... and more than that to always have open eyes and ears to understand when the Lord is passing nearby.'

In reply Ray Davey said, 'We know that there is no cheap and easy route to unity. We cherish and respect the separate traditions of each Church, but we are convinced that there are multitudes of things that are crying out to be done together, and it is high time we got on with them ... We are open to all people of good will who are willing to meet each other and to work together for the good of all.'[29]

It was a tall order, but Corrymeela swiftly 'got on with it'. The first major event with a high profile was an Easter meeting in 1966 when Prime Minister Terence O'Neill made a major speech to a large gathering of Protestants and Catholics at Corrymeela. The theme was 'Community 1966', the year which marked the fiftieth anniversary of two major events in 1916 – the Battle of the Somme, when almost a generation of young Ulstermen perished, and the Easter Rising in Dublin. As my Irish history professor J. C. Beckett once noted, 'Ireland was quickly passing under the most dangerous of all tyrannies – the tyranny of the dead.'[30]

O'Neill made his speech on the evening of Good Friday while security forces guarded the building outside in the driving rain. At the end of his challenging speech he made the strong appeal, 'If we cannot be united in all things, let us at least be united in working together in a Christian spirit to create better opportunities for our children ... as we advance to meet the promise of the future, let us shed the burdens of traditional grievances and ancient resentments. It must – and God willing – it will be done.'

This was a brave start for Corrymeela, and O'Neill's remarks received widespread publicity. People at Corrymeela were showing 'the audacity to hope', a term used later by Nelson Mandela about his own country, but sadly all too soon the framework for peace in Northern Ireland began to break down. Many people and institutions were overtaken by the torrent of violence, but Corrymeela was neither overwhelmed nor overcome. It was time to demonstrate to the world the practicalities of peacemaking.

The candle of hope flickering at Corrymeela was threatened by the violence all around, but the community opened its doors near Ballycastle to welcome people from all backgrounds who were seeking refuge. They included those from troubled areas near the flashpoints, who could benefit from a respite from the violence, and also meet others from different backgrounds.

Some of the quotes from those who took part still shock me when I read them in my first book on Corrymeela, which was published nearly fifty years ago. A young girl called Deirdre, who witnessed some fierce fighting in Belfast, said, 'I like Corrymeela and Ballycastle. I saw a lot of shops and none of them were burnt out.' Jimmy, who took part in a mixed-school project at Corrymeela, said when he came back home, 'At first I was scared. I was told before I went that I might get a good kicking from "the other side". But we found out that the other boys were just like us, and we liked them.' Another little girl called Mary wrote to Corrymeela to thank them and said, 'It really was a wonderful time. I changed my attitude to teachers, and to Protestants.'[31]

I remember visiting Corrymeela to report on a Family Week for the *Belfast Telegraph*. The place was lively, the noise was deafening, and it required hearts of lions from the volunteers who were dealing with excited and energetic young people, most of whom were away from home for the first time. I asked one of the helpers how she coped. I will always remember her reply. 'Back in my home in Belfast I go into my front parlour after teatime every day. My family know that this is my quiet time and that I don't want to be disturbed, because that is when I pray.'

Over the years, Corrymeela ran countless Family Weeks, seminars and all kinds of events in its beautiful hilltop sanctuary. It rapidly gained a high reputation for authenticity and impartiality in doing its good work. This was well described by a former Archbishop of Canterbury, Dr Donald Coggan, after an all too brief visit. He watched a small city boy hugging a lamb, and he observed, 'His world was a world of stones and guns and fire and slaughter. Corrymeela had brought him out from that, to meet with others of his own age and older to discover that whatever their label, Protestant or Catholic, they were human beings, and to glimpse perhaps that they, like him, were made in the image of God.'

The Corrymeela Community received recognition and practical support from other inter-community centres in Ireland, the UK and much further afield, and it welcomed many distinguished visitors, including, at different times, Mother Teresa and the Dalai Lama.

I recall particularly the Dalai Lama, whom I met in Belfast at a pre-arranged news conference prior to his visit to Ballycastle. I arrived at the conference about half an hour early, so I had him all to myself apart from one of his minders. Both of them wore big brown shoes and they giggled a lot, but they also listened intently. I explained to the Dalai Lama about the work of Corrymeela, and he told me the story of a fellow monk who had been imprisoned for ten years in Tibet by the Chinese authorities on trumped-up charges. He said, 'When my friend was released I asked him if he was bitter about those who had imprisoned him and he replied, "If I hold bitterness that will not harm my captors, but it will harm me."' When the Dalai Lama visited Corrymeela two days later he told Ray Davey and his colleagues, 'My spirit is with you, and please carry on your work tirelessly. You can consider me a member of your Community.'

The many events that took place in Corrymeela were organised for people of all ages and from all backgrounds, but the central theme was clearly emphasised by Ray Davey after a decade. He told a rededication service in 1975, 'We are not a social welfare body, nor a Community Relations project, nor a Community Development team, nor is this place a Conference House or a Holiday Centre. We are above all else a group of Christians who are trying to follow Christ and to do what he wants done in our society. We are disciples and therefore we accept the discipline of Christ.'[32]

During the years when I worked closely with Corrymeela to tell their story in a book and in many newspaper and other articles, I came to know Ray Davey well as a friend. He was a good listener and a role model who did not preach or appear 'holy'. Occasionally he would slip a book into my pocket saying, 'You might find this helpful'. I remember him giving me a paperback containing some of the lectures of the theologian Paul Tillich. I am not big into theology or theologians, but I still benefit from reading that book.

Shortly after I finished the Corrymeela book I travelled with Ray to New York in an attempt to raise funds. It was the only time I saw him really angry because he thought that a certain person had taken him for granted and had organised a meeting badly, a meeting that he had agreed to address. It reminded me of the righteous anger of Jesus driving the money-changers out of the Temple.

During our visit to New York we had dinner in a fashionable restaurant with my beloved uncle, Bill McCreary, who was high up in the food business there. I ordered a Rusty Nail aperitif, a ferocious mixture of Scotch and Drambuie. Ray was amused by the title, and for ever after, when he met me in company back home, he would ask with a wink, 'How are the rusty nails?' We never told anyone about our secret.

After one of Ray's visits abroad he and I went over to Rathlin Island and, after returning to the Corrymeela Centre, we sat outside the building and watched the sun go down. Ray was very quiet, and then he said to me pensively, 'The penny has to drop some time that reconciliation is what Christianity is all about. If we Christians cannot speak the message of reconciliation, who can? Otherwise we have nothing to say.'

Unfortunately the Irish Churches were part of the problem. Personal salvation seemed more important than social justice. The Catholic Church was identified with Irish Nationalism and the Protestant Churches with Unionism. There was little or no effort, until later, to bridge that gap. Tony Spencer, a sociologist from Queen's University, claimed that most Protestants, like most Catholics, had been unaware how their actions and those of their parents and grandparents had secularised Christianity in Ireland. He said, 'They desecrate daily in good conscience.'

Of course there were exceptions, and many individuals were reaching across the divides with prayer and with fine examples of Christian principles in their daily lives. In general, however, it was not easy for Corrymeela to be accepted by many members of the main Churches, who were unsure about ecumenism and reaching out to 'the other side'. Gradually, however, ecumenism started to take root, albeit patchily. Later on Ray Davey was awarded an honorary degree from Maynooth, one of the first Protestants to receive such an honour. He was also awarded an honorary degree by the Presbyterian Church in Ireland, which took long enough to accept that he was one of their most significant figures of the twentieth century.

Ray Davey and his early colleagues set out the principles that have sustained Corrymeela throughout almost six decades during which they carried the torch for greater understanding within the wider community. It would be wrong to suggest, however, that this was the only source of such work. Throughout the Troubles many secular institutions, including governments in the British Isles, Europe, the US and elsewhere, poured time, effort and expertise into encouraging better community relations and searching for a path towards a lasting peace.

A good example is Sir Tony O'Reilly, the co-founder with Dan Rooney of the Ireland Fund in 1976. The fund, of which Sir

Anthony is a former chairman, raised very large sums to help with cross-community and cultural projects at a time when huge amounts of money were also being raised in the US to help fund armed Republicanism in Ireland. During an interview for my book *Tried by Fire* he said, 'It is totally unChristian to seek a military solution. I am as proud of the Northern Irish as the Southern Irish, and to me it is a running sore that I have to protest my identity as an Irishman through the misunderstanding that the world has of Ireland, brought about largely by the viciousness of the tribal struggle.

'Those who argue the more tedious politics of peace find that it can be difficult to attract the attention of overworked politicians, whereas a well-placed bomb can create world attention. But the long term is the only way we can play the game, the boring game of peace.'[33]

Another individual who impressed me enormously was Dr Brendan O'Regan, a fine human being and a distinguished Irish businessman who founded Co-Operation North, now known as Co-Operation Ireland. One of the aims was to promote better understanding between institutions and people in similar fields, including business and commerce, and indeed in all fields where they could work within a common objective. He once told me, 'You have to have faith, which is another word for optimism. Faith, hope and charity, all three. The driving force in all of this is Christianity, though sometimes we are very unwilling and afraid to recognise this.'[34]

Another outstanding contribution to creating better community relations came from the International Fund for Ireland (IFI), established in 1986 by the British and Irish governments with financial help from the US, the European Union, Canada, Australia and New Zealand. The total funding by 2022 was £728/€914 million, for 6,000 shared projects across Ireland. When writing a book for the IFI I reported on a large number of these inspiring projects that brought ordinary people together – particularly in Irish border regions and in flashpoints in towns and cities elsewhere.

There were other smaller-scale but nevertheless important initiatives, such as the Dutch-Northern Ireland Foundation, which was funded by the Dutch Council of Churches. A large number of conferences were held in the Netherlands and attended by all kinds of groups and individuals from Northern Ireland. Among the leaders were the Reverend Aat van Rhijn, a Dutch Presbyterian, and Fr Andre Lascaris, a Dominican. They said, 'The original idea was to take people out of the situation and allow them to meet together in peace and quiet in Holland because many of them could not do this back home. We also wanted them to look back on Northern Ireland from a distance.'

I took part in a number of these conferences and I found them most worthwhile in helping to make people from Northern Ireland view their situation from different and perhaps more helpful perspectives. I remember particularly one conference involving Catholic and Protestant clerics, and I realised how many of them were badly overworked and needed a break. The Dutch hosts wanted them to work through the entire weekend but I voiced their desire to spend some time in Amsterdam. So I was invited to take them there myself and to look after them. There was much relaxation, and also a little dark humour. A couple of the Catholic priests were shopping for souvenirs in a place which bizarrely also had a number of sex toys near the back. The priests asked me, 'What are these things for?', but I hadn't the nerve to tell them. In mitigation, that was in the Europe of a long time ago.

Many people ask if all these church and secular peace initiatives made any difference during the Troubles. There is no way of knowing the correct answer to this, but I believe strongly that without such good people working tirelessly for better understanding across so many areas, the situation would have been much, much worse.

One of the most heart-warming stories about new beginnings and forgiveness was told to me by Ray himself. In his *War Diaries*, Ray describes the devastation of the Allied bombing of Dresden near the end of the Second World War. He was a prisoner-of-war near Dresden, but he witnessed the devastation the next day. He wrote, 'Today I went down to Dresden and saw it all for myself. In the streets there is an unusual silence; few people about; scattered groups of British or Russian POWs leisurely working on the ruins. I felt strangely uncomfortable walking around the sorrows of this once beautiful city.'[35]

Some forty years later Ray and his charming wife Kathleen, who was his tower of strength, travelled to Dresden as part of a group from the British Council of Churches to witness the re-emergence of the city from the war-torn ruins. Ray spoke at a service in the Kreuzkirche, which had been badly damaged in the bombing of 1945 but re-opened ten years later. He reflected on that service and said, 'I felt very much that I was not only speaking for myself but for all my fellow prisoners who had been with me away back forty years ago. I believe that we in that service together were being visible signs of that peace and reconciliation and oneness that God wills.'

That evening Ray and Kathleen were guests at the famous Dresden Opera House and they were sitting beside a German lady and her husband who had been at the service earlier in the day in the church were Ray had spoken. During the Allied air raids in 1945, the man's mother, six-year-old brother and both grandparents had died. Ever since then he had been filled with hatred and bitterness towards those who had killed his relatives. He went to the service in the Kreuzkirche, where he had been confirmed as a child, and after he heard Ray Davey speak, he felt that something had happened to him. He broke down in tears and realised that he could now forgive.

That is a good example of the work of Ray Davey at home and abroad and how his reconciling work helped to break down barriers everywhere. I will never forget him or his wife Kathleen. When I was rereading one of my Corrymeela books many years after its publication, I noticed a simple inscription on the flyleaf. It read, 'To Alf with thanks for everything, signed Ray and Kathleen'.

I found that terribly moving, and I felt that it was me who should be thanking them for the privilege of sharing in their lives.

They were two of the most remarkable people whose friendship I treasured. There were two other wonderful people whom I came to know later on, but only after the enormous tragedy of yet another mass killing.

12

Enniskillen: Light from Darkness

One of the greatest atrocities of the Troubles took place on 8 November 1987, when a no-warning Provisional IRA bomb exploded at the cenotaph in Enniskillen as people were gathering there for the Remembrance Day ceremony. Eleven people died, including student nurse Marie Wilson, aged twenty, whose father Gordon was badly hurt in the blast. Ronnie Hill, a school teacher, was also severely injured, and died thirteen years later, after a long coma.

I first heard about the bomb on BBC Radio Ulster as I drove to Bessbrook to a special birthday party for my mother. As the gruesome details were revealed minute by minute I noticed, to my surprise, that my wife Hilary was crying beside me in the car. However, I was totally in the 'news journalist' mode and was wondering how the various networks would cover such a major story. It was only later in the day that the enormity of what had happened began to sink in. I had reported on many different killings and maimings as the Troubles unfolded, but this was entirely different. There was a cold, grim cloud of despair hanging over everything.

The bombing was condemned worldwide. UK Prime Minister Margaret Thatcher said that it was 'a blot on mankind'. It was also condemned by Irish Taoiseach Charles Haughey, who expressed 'horror, anger and revulsion' on behalf of 'every decent Irish man and Irish woman'. Pope John Paul II declared his 'profound shock'. US President Ronald Reagan expressed his revulsion and noted 'the very cruel irony that such a deed should be done on a Day of Remembrance'. The bombing was even condemned by Moscow.

However, it was an interview with Gordon Wilson the next morning on BBC Radio which really knocked me back. He described the horror and shock of lying under the rubble of a bombed and demolished wall beside Marie, and how they held hands. Then her voice changed, and she said, 'Daddy, I love you very much.' Those were her last words.

Later that night Gordon told a BBC reporter, 'I have lost my daughter and I shall miss her. But I bear no ill will. I bear no grudge. Dirty sort of talk is not going to bring her back to life. She was a great wee lassie. She loved her profession. She was a pet. She's dead. She's in Heaven and we shall meet again. Don't ask me please for a purpose. I don't have a purpose. I don't have an answer. But I know there has to be a plan. If I didn't think that I would commit suicide. It's part of a greater plan, and God is good. And we shall meet again.'[36]

As I listened to Gordon I sat rooted to the spot. Those were the most harrowing and yet most noble words I had ever heard from any of the victims of the violence, even from the many people I had interviewed for the *Belfast Telegraph* and for my book *Tried By Fire*.

Gordon Wilson's reaction was all the more remarkable because it was unrehearsed and came straight from the heart. However, those words catapulted that humble Enniskillen draper into the world headlines in the immediate aftermath of the bombing, and for years afterwards. Gordon, whether he wanted to or not, became a media personality.

Though he was often a man of few words, Gordon had a natural gift for producing good sound bites, which suited every journalist or news presenter looking for a simple quote to sum up a complex situation. Gordon told me that he had once asked the then British Labour Party leader Neil Kinnock if he could ever go back to being just Gordon Wilson, the 'wee draper from the wee town'. Kinnock looked hard at him and said, 'You will never get back to being the Gordon Wilson you were.' That shook him, and Gordon said, 'He was absolutely right. It was as if someone had suddenly opened a window on the future and I saw what I had known already deep down in my subconscious, but which possibly I did not want to admit to. I could never go back, because the bomb had changed everything.'[37]

Though I later wrote extensively about the Wilson family, I did not meet Gordon for quite some time after the events of 8 November 1987. Two days after the bombing I travelled to the Somme battlefields of the First World War with a community group from North Belfast to mark the 11 November 1918 Armistice at a moving ceremony at the Thiepval Tower. It was a dark morning, which matched the sombre mood of those French and Northern Irish people who took part in the ceremony. As the reality of such mass slaughter in the past hung over us, I could not help thinking of the slaughter at the Enniskillen Cenotaph only a few days previously, when people came to pay their respects to their war dead. The crushing litany of violence at home and abroad seemed unending.

About a year after my return to Belfast I had a phone call from the manager of the publishing company which had produced a book of mine on the victims of violence. She asked if I would be interested in helping Gordon Wilson to write a book about Marie. I agreed to help, and then put the phone down. Nothing happened for some time and I thought that I should perhaps ring Gordon myself to talk him into doing something. However, I felt that this was not the right motive. Who was I to talk to a man who had suffered so much in order to try to interest him in something that I wanted to do? I put it out of my mind completely.

Another year passed, and then I had a phone call telling me that Gordon needed help, and asking me if I was still prepared to talk to him. A few days later we met for the first time in a hotel midway between Belfast and Dungannon. Gordon strode in briskly, a tall and gangly man with a bone-crushing handshake and an air of no-nonsense integrity. We immediately took to one another and we agreed to start working on the book as soon as possible. This was the start of one of the most moving and inspiring challenges of my writing career.

We quickly established a suitable working schedule, whereby I would travel to Enniskillen every weekend to interview Gordon and his wife Joan, a wonderful, strong Christian woman. As I talked to both of them in depth I began to put together the real story behind all the earlier headlines.

I soon realised the toll that the bomb and the loss of Marie had taken on Gordon. He had been badly injured with a dislocated shoulder and severe bruising. There were also the considerable personal challenges facing a man who had been brutally pushed into the spotlight. He told me that he had talked to the BBC reporter on the night of the bomb because he felt that 'this story' needed to be told to the world. He never wanted to be a 'spokesman' for Enniskillen, and he and Joan were always conscious that so many other people had died or had been injured in the explosion.

I had not realised beforehand that Gordon had to be aware of so many local sensitivities. A few days after the bombing he attended a memorial service in the local Catholic church where, to his amazement, the people in the packed congregation applauded him as he walked up the aisle. He said, 'I was totally flabbergasted. Later that week some people asked why I had gone to the Catholic service. I answered them by saying that something inside told me that the Catholic people of Enniskillen were making an important gesture to all the families of the eleven who had died. They were willing to pray for us, and to extend the hands of friendship and love. They were saying in an even deeper sense, "We are truly SORRY." I felt very deeply that the warmth of response from my Catholic neighbours was important and that I had to share with them.'

In December 1987 the Queen paid tribute to Gordon in her Christmas broadcast. She said, 'From time to time we see some inspiring examples of tolerance. Mr Gordon Wilson impressed the whole world by the depths of his forgiveness. His strength and that of his wife, and the courage of their daughter came from their Christian conviction.' This unusual step of mentioning people by name gave further massive publicity to Gordon, who received many accolades, including a World Methodist Peace Award. Yet he was never totally happy with such personal recognition, because so many others had suffered too. After a poll on BBC Radio 4 he was named Man of the Year, ahead of the Russian leader Mikhail Gorbachev and Prince Charles. He told me later, 'In my heart of hearts I knew that I could not be compared with such men. They were on the world's stage, and I was just the man from Enniskillen. On the other hand I was aware that if someone was giving me an award or an accolade it would have been churlish to refuse because it was on behalf of many others also that I was receiving such attention.'[38]

As I carried out my weekend interviews I gradually came to realise that Gordon was not the man he had been physically. After the bomb and Marie's funeral, he went into a period of deep mourning, which also affected his health. He kept watching the news recordings about the bomb and its aftermath until his family took them away from him. He told me that he gradually began to lose interest in his drapery business, whereas he had previously enjoyed the strong competition of this trade. He also realised that he did not have as much energy as before. At one point he began behaving strangely and lost his memory. His daughter Julie-Anne thought he was 'losing his marbles'. He was admitted to the local hospital for a short period, but he recovered relatively quickly from his brief lapse, which had been caused by stress.

Despite this worrying setback he maintained a challenging schedule of public appearances, talks and broadcasts as the media and others continually asked him about his 'forgiveness' of those who had murdered Marie. It was this concept, however, that proved to be one of the big challenges for me in helping him to write the book. Over lunch one day I said to him, 'The media often refer to your forgiveness, but you never said that you forgave the bombers. You said that you bore no ill will, but that is not the same thing.'

After a long pause he replied, 'You are right. Their crime was so heinous that only God can forgive them, if they repent. For my part I still bear no ill will, and I pray for them every night.' I like to think that somehow Gordon's prayers may have softened him into a form of forgiveness. I always respected him for his views on that difficult subject and I also feel that I owe him a debt for such an example. When I find it hard to forgive someone I remember Gordon's words, and I then work hard not to bear any ill will in the expectation that I too may soften into the forgiveness of others.

One of the major developments in Gordon's later life was Taoiseach Albert Reynolds's offer in February 1993 of a seat in the Irish Senate. Gordon feared that some of his fellow Unionists in the Enniskillen area would not approve. He was right, and he faced criticism in public and more strongly in private, but he went ahead anyway. He greatly enjoyed his time in the Senate, and as a good raconteur he liked telling stories about some of the many characters there. He also loved being in Dublin, where he had spent his schooldays at Wesley College.

He also proved to be politically adept in his new role. My old friend Austin Currie worried that Gordon might be too naive in the tough world of politics. 'He told me he was naive and I realised that he was not so naive after all. He was very shrewd, and a great deal shrewder than many people gave him credit for.'

Tom Garvin, Professor of Politics at University College Dublin, who helped Gordon with some of his speeches, saw him as a 'wily old bird who could use his situation to great political effect'. Albert Reynolds said that if Gordon had turned down his offer of the Senate seat he would not have known where to go next. 'He was a man with a message and he did not have to respond to situations in the same way as politicians do. He was a free agent. I would not have got anyone else to fill that Senate post in the way he filled it.'[39]

It was during Gordon's time in the Irish Senate that he took the significant step of asking to meet the Provisional IRA to find out if they were working to end their violence. In doing so he stressed to them that he recognised that people on all sides had lost loved ones, but he made it clear that the actions and excuses of those who murdered Marie and the others were in no way justifiable. However, he felt that as Marie's father he had a moral claim to be taken seriously by them.

Several days later the Provisionals confirmed that they would meet Gordon, and some weeks after that he met their representatives at a house in Donegal after a journey along twisted roads, blindfolded, that disoriented him totally. He was taken to a bungalow and was received politely by a man and a young woman. A third person was present to take notes. The Provisionals immediately handed him a typed statement, which they said would be issued to the media afterwards. It seemed to Gordon as if they had made up their minds already.

His instinct was not far wrong. During the encounter he talked about the widespread suffering as a result of the Provisional IRA bombs in Enniskillen and elsewhere, but he felt that his listeners were unmoved. One of them conceded that Gordon was indeed sincere, but that it was 'naive to think that the IRA holds the key to peace'. Gordon replied, 'You are blaming the Brits. I have heard this a thousand times.'

The meeting dragged on but it ended in an impasse. Gordon was driven back to Donegal town to pick up his own car and he returned to Enniskillen wearily, and in despair. Back home he kept saying, 'There will never be peace in this country.' His daughter Julie-Anne said, 'He was in a terrible state and totally shocked by the IRA's response.' Gordon said later, 'The bottom line for me was peace but I got nothing. Perhaps I was duped.'[40]

Significantly, however, he felt better for some time after the meeting. A burden had been lifted after many months of worrying, and he was more at peace with himself. Some sixteen months later he took some consolation from the announcement of a Provisional IRA ceasefire on 31 August 1994. Perhaps his face-to-face encounter with the Provisionals in Donegal had not been entirely in vain.

Gordon continued to make a valuable contribution to the Irish Senate and to the Forum for Peace and Reconciliation, which had been set up by the Dublin government shortly after the announcement of the Provisional IRA ceasefire. Gordon told me later that he had an altercation during a closed session of the Forum with one of the Provisional IRA leaders, Martin McGuinness, who accused the Royal Ulster Constabulary of much wrongdoing against the Irish Nationalist community in Northern Ireland and demanded their disestablishment. Gordon interrupted him to say that he would not listen to these unchallenged comments from a man whose associates had killed his daughter. Afterwards McGuinness apologised to Gordon and said that his remarks had not been personal to his family. Gordon appreciated the gesture from someone he regarded as 'a hard man', and they shook hands. Perhaps Gordon was seeing a glimpse of the 'other' Martin McGuinness, who amazed everyone years later by agreeing to share power at Stormont with the Reverend Ian Paisley.[41] Austin Currie, an observer at the Forum, said that Sinn Féin always listened carefully to Gordon. 'He was always one up on them because everyone knew that the IRA had killed his daughter.'

Despite the stresses of his public role in the Irish Senate and elsewhere, Gordon seemed to be emerging from under some of the darkest clouds of the past. One afternoon in November 1994 I almost literally bumped into him outside the Irish parliament in Dublin and he invited me inside for a cup of tea. He was in great form, and my heart lifted for him.

Then, a month later, on 7 December Gordon's world was brutally shattered again, this time by the death of his son Peter, who was killed in a car accident just outside Enniskillen. He was only thirty-eight years old, and this was almost beyond belief. Madeleine Taylor-Quinn, a Senate colleague, was the first to hear the awful news from Gordon that evening. She said, 'I could not believe that this man, who was forced in the past to bear such heartbreak, sadness and grief, was being asked to carry another major burden. Yet I had to be impressed by the manner, dignity and grace with which he carried the news and the way he made arrangements to get back to Joan.[42]

A few days later my wife Hilary and I went to Peter's funeral in Enniskillen, and we were invited to the family home beforehand. Gordon appeared normal, but I knew that inside he was agitated and he seemed not to be himself. Peter's death had hit him very hard. He had been through so much and he had coped with so much, but this latest family tragedy broke his heart. Just over seven months or so later he died from a stroke on 27 June 1995 at his home in Enniskillen. He was sixty-seven. It was a sunny morning and he went upstairs to rest, because, as ever, he had been setting himself a punishing pace. It was a quick and peaceful death for a man who had known so much pain, but sadly he died alone. Joan was at a conference in Galway and Julie-Anne was driving down from Moira to Enniskillen in her mother's car, which she had borrowed.

Gordon's funeral service in Darling Street Methodist Church, which had also witnessed the funeral services of his daughter Marie and son Peter, was packed with a large congregation from all over Ireland, including President Mary Robinson, a friend of his, and also Albert Reynolds, who had appointed him to the Irish Senate. The representation from Northern Unionism was disappointing, but there was a large turnout of people from all backgrounds who wanted to pay their respects.

In the hot summer temperatures all the men were sitting with their jackets off, and the sombre funeral service seemed surreal on such a bright, sunny day. It was hard to believe that Gordon, this man of light and hope, was dead. There was an air of great loss and sadness, not only for the family, but for a person who had achieved so much. In the biblical sense he had indeed 'fought a good fight, he had finished his course and he had kept the faith'. He had done so with grace, courage and dignity, and with total commitment to his deep Christian roots, which had sustained him throughout his life right to the very end. He was an ordinary man who thought of himself as 'the wee draper from Enniskillen', but in reality he became an extraordinary hero in the darkest of times. I still feel blessed to have known him and to have been considered by him as a friend, and also to have been such a close friend of Joan, his wife and steadfast pillar of support. She too deserves to have her own remarkable story told.

13

A Tower of Strength

Joan Watson and Gordon Wilson were married on 2 August 1955 in a small Methodist church in Fermanagh, and they set up home in a flat over the Wilson family's drapery shop in the centre of Enniskillen.

They were both strong characters. Joan was a clever woman, a talented musician from farming stock who later became a music teacher, and Gordon was a born businessman. They were a happy couple and made a good marriage. Gordon was a man of his time, when women were not expected to make their own careers until after the children were reared.

Joan began teaching early on but resigned when their son Peter was born. She could not bear to leave him at home. Later on she went back to teaching and was Head of Music at Enniskillen Collegiate School. She also was the organist and choir-mistress at Enniskillen Methodist Church for many years.

When Peter was nearly two, their second son Richard died very shortly after his birth. Joan was so ill that she was not allowed to see him. Many weeks later, when she was stronger, Gordon took her to see Richard's grave. She told me, 'It was terrible. Even though it happened a long time ago, a great feeling of sadness comes over me when I think of what might have been. I don't think that people get over the premature death of a baby.'

Many people regarded Gordon Wilson as a saint, but he was reassuringly human and not always saintly. Joan told me that people would say to her, 'Your husband is a beautiful man.' She would reply, 'I'll be the judge of that. I live with him!' She said, 'Of course he was a beautiful person but he could lose his temper, and he was impatient and always in a rush. He was always very competitive in sport. He was a member of the Ireland fishing team, and even when he played badminton he was aggressive. Gordon was not a good loser! I asked myself – was this the man I married?

'It was the same with golf. When he played badly he came home depressed. I used to get fed up with these post-mortems and they became worse as he got older. I said to him, "You would think you were playing in the Ryder Cup." He hated domestic chores and gardening but he took great pride in the lawn. He would say to me, "Joan that lawn looks well after it is cut." I would ask him, "Who trimmed the edges and the shrubs?"'

Nevertheless, Joan and the several 'Gordon Wilsons' lived happily with one another. 'I knew before we were married that he was a churchgoer. I don't think there was ever a Damascus Road experience. But there was a gradual deepening of his faith. He taught me that love mattered, that you aired your views, and there were no secrets. There was love and trust, and as the years went on we got to know one another better and better. We were fortunate in that we were friends.[43]

'I was a dreamer, but he wakened me out of my dreams. I learned to be on time, to say what I really meant and not to be afraid of people. Above all he taught me the power of love. He often said "The bottom line is love", and he practised it all his life. He didn't preach but he showed love in the simple things.

'I remember as a young girl praying to God, in a way that might now seem silly, for the "right" young man to share my life. And the Lord did not let me down. Gordon and I went through so much together, and I don't know how we would have managed without each other. He was a wonderful husband and friend.'

They needed all their strength together on that awful day when Marie was murdered by the Provisional IRA bomb, and for the rest of their lives together.

On the day of the bomb, Joan was busy in the family kitchen when Gordon and Marie set off for the cenotaph. Joan called to Marie, 'Have you an umbrella?' She replied, 'Of course I have, don't fuss.' Those were the last words she said to her mother. Joan was still in the kitchen with Peter, who had called in for a coffee, when they heard the bomb go off. It sounded like a dull thud in the distance. They knew that Gordon and Marie were at the cenotaph, and they were desperately worried.

Later that morning Joan was playing the organ in the local Methodist church, but she could not settle. Her anxiety and fear were increasing rapidly. Meanwhile, Peter and his sister Julie-Anne had driven to the Erne Hospital. They met Gordon there, but there was no trace of Marie. Joan was taken to the hospital where she saw Gordon distressed and sitting in the Emergency Department in a wheelchair with a very painful dislocated shoulder. There was still no sign of Marie, but more than two hours later they were told that she was in Intensive Care.

Gordon could not move, but Joan and Julie-Anne went to Marie. She had very extensive injuries. Joan told me later about her last moments. 'I kissed her gently. Her face looked so different. There were scratches on her cheek. The doctor looked at us and shook his head sadly. I saw Marie's eyelids flicker. Then the ward sister said gently, "Marie's heart has stopped beating. It's all over now." Julie-Anne said, "Mum, it's better this way." I could only say the prayer "The Lord gave, the Lord has taken away, blessed be the name of the Lord." I looked back at Marie for a few last times, and then I had to go downstairs and tell Gordon that his darling daughter was dead.'[44]

As I write these words, coincidentally in the days before Remembrance Sunday 2023, I find myself welling up, and I have to stop writing for a while. After all these years the raw emotion has not gone away, and I still remember with total admiration and almost wondering disbelief the remarkable words of Joan just seconds after Marie's death. 'The Lord gave, the Lord has taken away, blessed be the name of the Lord.' That is a total faith in God, which almost goes beyond human understanding. As the father of two great sons, Mark and Matthew, and a beautiful daughter, Emma, I don't think I could have said that, and I doubt if many other parents could have done so either.

What is so utterly remarkable about Joan's immediate reaction in the hospital almost the second that Marie died, and Gordon's reaction on the night of the bombing, was their spontaneity. These were not the result of deep reflection, but simply the profoundly honest and instinctive reactions of two anguished people in their darkest moments who still clung to their deep belief and trust in God, whatever the circumstances. They gave a totally different dimension to the concept of 'keeping the faith', which to me still remains greatly humbling and inspiring all these years later.

Lord Eames, then the Church of Ireland Primate, was in Enniskillen that day to take part in a service of remembrance at the local cathedral, but he rushed to the Erne hospital to help as best he could. He said, 'The tragic and horrifying events will never be forgotten by those of us who were there. I spoke to Gordon and what he said and did were of infinitely greater significance and meaning than the bomb and the bullet. His words, his attitude, his sheer human goodness and faith shone out like a beacon of hope in the darkness.'[45]

Marie's funeral was held two days in the Enniskillen Methodist Church in the full glare of the media, though Gordon was clear that the family did not want any cameras inside the church, nor did they want any political comment. Joan recalled that Gordon had said, 'Let's get through this with as much dignity as we can'. 'That's what we tried to do. The service generated for me a great sense of peace. We were totally shattered, but the music, the readings and the prayers were very uplifting. On the way out the local Anglican bishop, the Rt Reverend Brian Hannon, touched Gordon's arm and said to him, "You are doing well." That meant a lot to Gordon. Julie-Anne was a tower of strength, even though she was breaking up inside. She was very, very upset, particularly after the funeral.'

In the aftermath the family had to gather themselves together as best they could. Gordon was still exhausted and frail. Even the most simple tasks became complicated. Joan had to wash Gordon's hair to get rid of the last traces of the dust from the rubble. In doing so she saw the bruises and discolouration of his skin and realised how much he had suffered physically.

She was churned up inside too. People who did not know her assumed that she shared the same views as Gordon when he told the media on the night of the bombing that he bore no 'ill will' towards his daughter's killers. Joan reminded me, 'I had a feeling of passionate anger, and that did not go away quickly or easily. It lasted through the funeral and for many months afterwards. I asked myself, 'How could the bombers look at themselves in the mirror after committing such unspeakable crimes? How could they do that to so many innocent people? I had to work hard at overcoming my anger. Gordon's words were a great help because I knew that he was right.'

However, Joan never gave up the search for justice for the people who had killed Marie and all the others. She also believed firmly that if they evaded justice in this world, they would face a greater Judge and judgement later on.

Some years later, when I helped Gordon to write his book on Marie, I came to know and to admire the Wilson family, and over the years Joan became one of my closest friends. I came to realise how much she had managed to hold herself and her family together through the darkest of times.

Joan was by Gordon's side during many of his extensive public engagements, but where possible she tried to stay in the background and gave very few media interviews, apart from speaking to me for the *Belfast Telegraph*. However, she was very helpful to the countless reporters from all over the world who came to interview Gordon at their home in Enniskillen. She said, 'I knew that they were only doing their job, and the least I could do was to bring them tea and biscuits.'

Joan also had an important mission of her own, and she went out of her way to meet others who had lost loved ones through the Troubles and to help them deal with their bereavement. She often brought with her a copy of the book about Marie and her own bereavement anthology, *All Shall Be Well*, which I helped her to compile. In this way she built up a very wide circle of friends.

She also met some very well-known people, including Queen Elizabeth, and Lady Diana, whom she admired greatly. I used to tease her about the way in which Diana outsmarted Prince Charles at every turn, but I believe that she had detected in Diana a deep empathy, which touched her heart.

On one occasion she invited me to join her and Julie-Anne at a ceremony in Westminster Abbey in memory of the civilian victims of worldwide violence, in the presence of Queen Elizabeth. We attended a reception afterwards in the Jerusalem Chamber, a medieval room where King Henry IV died in 1413, and where many committees met to compile the Authorized Version of the Bible of 1611, and subsequent versions.

Joan was rebuilding her life with great courage and purpose after Marie's death but she was plunged into despair again when Peter was killed and Gordon died suddenly some months later. Following Peter's death a deeply grieving Joan said, 'I used to think how great it was to have a big son like Peter to look after me. But it was not to be. I often asked myself why I was not allowed to have my son to take care of me in my old age.'

When Gordon died, Joan was in Galway. On her return to Enniskillen she dreaded the thought of seeing him lying dead on their bed, but equally she could not bear the thought of not seeing him. She said later, 'Once I entered the room that sense of dread left me. He was lying there, with a great air of peace. I said to him, "Gordon, dear, you have done your best. You have given your all for peace and reconciliation." I thanked God for all that Gordon had been to me and our children. I now had to struggle on, with the help of Julie-Anne and the others, but now he was at peace.'[46]

In the days, months and years after the funeral Joan grieved in private and she continued to keep the family together. She also brought comfort to others, but she never really got over the deaths of her husband and children. She always dreaded the days before the annual Remembrance Day service at the Enniskillen Cenotaph, and I remember talking to her at her home on a dark early November afternoon as she sat beside a framed picture of Marie. She said, 'People tell me that time heals the wounds, but it doesn't. It only teaches you how to cope. The pain is always there.'

Joan had to learn to cope in other ways, and she disliked people who referred to her as 'a poor widow'. She said, 'I never thought of myself like that. I have a wealth of riches all around me, my family, my friends, my neighbours and my music.' She was also hurt by people who asked, 'How are you?' and did not stop to listen. She said, 'It's often the people who have suffered themselves who are prepared to take time to listen to you because they know what suffering is like. The others don't even realise that you have already noticed that they don't really want to hear you.'[47]

As Joan slipped in to a more gentle old age she had the comfort and joy of a loving and extended wider family. She and I used to talk regularly by phone and meet at least once a year, when I was delighted to see some of the joy returning to her face. On one such occasion she asked me to speak at her funeral, and I readily agreed to do so, though I knew it would not be easy.

Sadly, she spent her last few months of her life in a long and difficult illness, and she died on 31 March 2023, aged ninety-one. Her family described her rightly as 'a remarkable woman', and two days later I paid a funeral tribute to her in front of a packed congregation in Enniskillen Methodist Church. It was a moving and also an inspiring occasion, and her family and I were touched by the wide range of people who had come to pay their last respects.

Later in the year I paid my final public tribute to Joan in an article for the *Belfast Telegraph*, which was published to mark the thirty-sixth anniversary of the Enniskillen bomb. I wrote, 'Her voice was a voice calling for justice for all the victims of violence, and she drew deeply from the bedrock of her strong Christian faith which had helped her to come through so much. Sadly that voice is no longer with us, but her shining example lives on to challenge and to inspire us towards seeking better days for everyone after so much suffering and distress.'

There was nothing more I could say or that could be said about one of the most inspiring and deeply Christian human beings I have ever met. Her words continued to comfort me when I had to report on large-scale violence elsewhere in the world, including Rwanda, which became the scene of mass slaughter almost beyond human comprehension. Yet, there also I discovered remarkable people who were keeping the faith in the most dire circumstances imaginable.

14

Father Teresa

'I make a distinction between tolerance and forgiveness. You can learn to tolerate someone who has harmed you, but forgiveness touches the heart. Forgiveness means that "I also have to love you." I feel that God has kept me alive and that I am living for a purpose. So I do try to forgive, but it's not easy.'

These words were spoken to me by a charming young woman called Claudette in the aftermath of the Rwandan genocide in 1994, when almost a million of the Tutsi minority were slaughtered by militants from the Hutu majority in around 100 days of tribal madness, while the major powers in the developed world, with cold political calculation, failed to intervene.

Claudette told me that her father, two brothers and two sisters were murdered during the genocide, and that she was severely traumatised. At only nineteen years of age she was abducted from her boarding school and taken to a holding centre where she was threatened with rape by a soldier and nearly killed. She was saved only by the intervention of the man's commanding officer. She managed to flee across the border to a Congolese refugee camp where she met some of her former attackers who were still hostile and told her that they regretted not having killed her.

She crossed back into Rwanda again and rebuilt her life. She gained impressive academic qualifications, raised a young family and worked as Executive Director for Moucecore, a Christian movement for evangelistic counselling and reconciliation. This organisation worked closely with churches across the religious divide to foster greater community development, supported by international agencies including the UK-based Tearfund Christian charity. In June 2019 Claudette formed her own Empowering Communities Initiative charity to help vulnerable and poor women, and so far she and her colleagues have helped to empower over 400 individuals.

It was during my visit to Rwanda and Uganda with a group from Tearfund several years ago that I met Claudette, who impressed me with her grace and deep Christian commitment. She said to me that she thought every day about her father and brothers and sisters who had been murdered. 'I don't know who killed them. I believe that they were Hutus but I cannot hate all Hutus. Perhaps if I met the killers I might be able to judge my forgiveness better. I also wonder how those people could have killed others who had not harmed them, and what life would like now for all of us if they had been allowed to live.'[48]

Claudette's words were similar to those of many victims of the Troubles whom I had interviewed back home in Northern Ireland, except that the scale of the killings was so much worse. My visit to the Kigali Genocide Museum was horrific, and there are no words to adequately describe it.

Nevertheless, violent death is death wherever you encounter it, when the prevailing political system has failed to provide a framework where people in a divided society can learn to live in peace. One of my most searing and yet inspiring interviews of all took place with a survivor of the Rwandan violence. As we talked in a building overlooking the Kigali prison where many of the Hutu killers were incarcerated I listened to a story that I could scarcely believe.

Michael, a Tutsi school teacher, lost fifty-six members of his family in the genocide. He had to go on the run from his Hutu pursuers, who chased him with dogs into the forest. Fortunately he found shelter in the homes of Hutus as he moved from place to place. Finally, he was taken in by a Hutu woman who gave him shelter for several weeks. One day he said to her, 'The time will come when my attackers will knock on your front door to get me. I will walk out alone, but you must stay hidden or they will kill you too.'

She replied, 'I could not do that. What would the angels say to me in Heaven when I tell them that I had abandoned you in your hour of greatest need? I will stay with you to the very end.' Inevitably the loud knocking on her door did come. Michael and the woman opened it slowly and fearfully, expecting the worst, but instead of confronting their would-be killers they were rescued by French paratroopers.

Michael told me long afterwards, 'We are all children of God and we need to come out from our ethnic mindsets and to repent and to forgive, in order to transform our society.' His remarkable words and brave Christian example were an object lesson for the people of my own country, who are still struggling to come to terms fully with our own tortured past.

My visit to Rwanda was long before the country became involved in a controversy about dealing with immigrants from the UK and elsewhere. During my time there I met so many people from both the Hutu and Tutsi communities who were working together to build friendships and to try to establish reconciliation after the horrors of the past. I returned to Northern Ireland with an even deeper awareness of how much we still had to learn from people in other countries. I was also aware that a deep Christian faith helped many of them to work together for a better future for everyone.

This was not my first visit to the developing world, though my involvement in writing about such subjects is a story in itself. At the height of the Troubles, with bombs going off regularly, I had a phone call. The Reverend Ian McDowell from the Belfast office of Christian Aid, the British Churches overseas relief and development agency, asked me if I could write a story for the upcoming Christian Aid week. The request seemed to me to come from a different world, as I was busy reporting on the aftermath of a bomb that had just exploded. So I declined his offer, though I felt a bit guilty about doing so.

The next Sunday I listened to a sermon by the Reverend Fergie Marshall in my own Whitehouse Presbyterian Church and he challenged us by suggesting that we should help Christian Aid with our time and our talents, and not just by putting money on the collection plate, which was so often the easy option. So a few days later I wrote a story for the *Belfast Telegraph* about Christian Aid, and it brought a huge response from our readers, who sent in large sums of money to help.

Even some of my allegedly 'hard-bitten' journalistic colleagues were also impressed, and they suggested that if someone would take up a weekly collection they would also donate to Christian Aid. That person, not surprisingly, was me, as no one else offered, but I was happy to oblige.

I was impressed not only by the generosity of my readers and colleagues, but also by the fact that this outreach to others was taking place at a time when Northern Ireland and its people were trapped in a deadly quagmire of violence and political deadlock. This inspired me to write to Christian Aid headquarters in the UK to offer help, though I stressed that I could not work in London for family reasons. It must have been one of the most well-meaning but perhaps naive letters I ever wrote, but to my great surprise they offered me an eight-month contract to travel around the developing world to report on their work, provided I could take the time off from the *Belfast Telegraph*. Roy Lilley, to my grateful delight, gave me a sabbatical, which was unheard of in Belfast journalism in those days.

Soon enough I embarked for Africa, Asia and Latin-America on a journey that troubled and inspired me, and one that I will never forget. My *Belfast Telegraph* colleagues gave me a warm send-off reception during which one of them asked, 'How are you travelling to London?' I said innocently, 'By British Airways', to which he replied, 'Oh, I thought you were walking on the water', and they all fell about laughing at my expense. Another colleague called out, 'Have a good trip, Father Teresa'. I loved that, and just being one of them.

This led to a book called *Up With People*, and to regular visits to the developing world for the next three decades or so, first with Christian Aid and later with Tearfund. Back home I also fulfilled regular speaking engagements in churches and with other groups of people to tell them about Christian Aid and to help raise funds.

I still regard these visits as some of the most fulfilling and inspiring of my professional career. I met countless people living in very poor circumstances who were also rich human beings. Many, though not all, were Christians, and I marvelled at how their faith seemed to sustain them in the most dire circumstances. I often discovered that many of the people who were constantly on the edge of death were also very much alive spiritually. I learned a great deal about my own lifestyle back in the developed world, and how much I and others took our gifts for granted.

In the Sudan, for example, I had lunch with a French engineer who was helping to build concrete boats for a Christian Aid project. I ordered roast lamb in a small roadside restaurant. When it was served it was covered in flies. I immediately decided to send it back but the French engineer said to me, 'Just brush off the dead flies and eat it, because that's all they have to serve you.' I brushed off the flies, ate the meat and survived.

In India I met a young Anglican ordinand who had given up a lucrative career in finance to join the ministry. I told him how much I admired his choice, and asked him what kind of work of was doing. He told me that on the previous day he had visited one of the many extensive slums in Mumbai and had asked a man lying there, 'How are you?' The man started crying and said, 'You are the only person who has ever asked me how I feel.'

In Dar-es-Salaam in Tanzania I went to a service in a Moravian church, where the large congregation were saying goodbye to a young cleric who was being transferred to a rural area. It was fascinating to watch female members of the church glide gracefully up the aisle to give him small presents on behalf of the congregation. Finally, they brought up their greatest present, which was a pushbike. On seeing it, the young cleric burst into tears. In

Tanzania getting that bike was like getting a Mercedes back in the developed world.

In Chile I went to an evangelical service in a rural area where the Christian leader was helping to set up a new church. He was overjoyed when people presented him with a collection of large pots and pans, which would prove essential for the church's catering needs. On the wall of the modest building I noted a message in Spanish which reminded me that 'The Lord is My Shepherd' – one of my favourite verses from the Bible. In that small church I was again reminded of the universality of the Christian message, and of the people from so many different backgrounds still keeping the faith with gratitude and joy, whatever their circumstances.

During a later visit to South Africa I went to a little church near Ladysmith where the local women had gathered for a meeting. It was a small humble dwelling with an earthen floor, which many people back home would describe as a shack, but the enthusiasm and Christian witness of the native women were so impressive they would have filled a large cathedral in the developed world. Later in my visit I met people in challenging circumstances to which there were no easy answers, and which tested their faith to the uttermost.

At a conference of clerics near Johannesburg they were discussing the challenge of officiating at so many funerals of people who had died from Aids. Someone suggested that they should hold a conference to consider 'the theology of compassion'. I suggested politely that all they needed to do was to read the parable of the Good Samaritan. I am still not sure that my suggestion was well received.

On an earlier visit to Africa the story of the Good Samaritan was all too real for me. I had been scheduled to travel from the Sudan to Nigeria but at the last moment Christian Aid switched me to Tunisia. At Khartoum Airport my traveller's cheque was rejected by an excited and overbearing bank teller because it was 'the wrong colour of paper', and I arrived with hardly any money in Cairo, en route to Tunis. Somehow I found a place for an overnight stay in Cairo, and the next day I arrived early at the airport for my flight to Tunisia. At the ticket desk I was having difficulty with my schoolboy French, when a man behind me said, 'Don't worry, I will handle this.' He sorted out my details, and we sat together on the plane. My helper was Frank McGuinness, a French-Canadian who had been on a business trip to Iraq, and was returning home. On our plane journey high above the African desert, where my old friend Ray Davey had been captured by the German army during the Second World War, my new acquaintance Frank and I shared our stories.

As we approached Tunis airport close to midnight, I asked Frank for a lift to the city centre as I only had an uncashed cheque and therefore no ready money for a taxi. I also had no idea where I would stay. However, the taxi passed through the centre of the city and ended up outside the five-star Hilton Hotel on the outskirts of Tunis.

Frank jumped out, entered the hotel, and came back shortly to tell me, 'I have booked you a room for the night.' I replied, 'Frank, my Christian Aid budget could not possibly afford that', but he said, 'Don't worry, buddy, this is for your cause. The cost is on me.'

I have never forgotten that, and never will. This was the story of the Good Samaritan, and I was the person who badly needed help. It also made me think of how the victim in the Good Samaritan story must have felt. In my case I wanted to repay Frank in some way, and later I was able to send him a book I had written about the work of the hospitals and the medical and nursing professions during the Troubles back home. This was intended as a present for his father who was a surgeon in Canada.

There are enough stories from my time in the developing world to make a book in itself. I will always be grateful for being given the opportunities to help, and to learn from those Christians, and people of other faiths, whose lives were so impressive in some of the most appalling circumstances imaginable. I also felt a strong sense of obligation in fulfilling so many speaking and other engagements at home in order to spread the message.

I particularly remember returning from Tunis to London halfway through my first major trip with Christian Aid. It was Christmas time and I decided to attend the Sunday morning service at Westminster Abbey. As I entered that beautiful place of worship with its ornate trappings, I thought about my tough journeys in Africa during the previous weeks and I asked myself, 'What will the preacher say to me this morning that speaks to my disturbing inner questions about justice, affluence and poverty the world over?' The speaker was Canon Colin Semper, and he began his sermon by saying, 'I want to talk to you about four of the most important words in the Gospel – they are "The Word became flesh!"' That was good enough for me.

My work in the developing world has been a privilege, but it still makes me angry about the continuing deadlock back home, about the waving of flags and emblems, the pompous self-importance of so many people from both sides, their lack of vision in not electing politicians who could make peace, their self-justification, the 'whataboutery', and in so many cases their bloody-mindedness in always looking to the past and not to the future. I have often thought that if our people on all sides were transported to parts of Africa, Asia or Latin-America, and had to live with the harsh challenges that those people have to face every day, they would come back to this beautiful island and peacefully share its riches in so many different ways.

My experiences from the developing world have also led me to despair at times, because there is still so much to be done. However, I am a writer and not a politician, and I try to take comfort from the knowledge that while I cannot change the world, my work may have helped others to change one person's world.

I have also reflected many times on how my work in the developing world took place at all, from the most unpromising circumstances. Was it all a coincidence, or did the all doors open unexpectedly because I was perhaps marching to the sound of a different drum? I will leave that for others to decide, but I still wrestle with that question, which runs like a thread throughout my career.

I have so many good memories of the people I met during my visits to the developing world, and I still keep in touch with Claudette from Rwanda, who recovered from the trauma of her abduction and sexual assault during the genocide. Since then she has devoted her time and energy to doing good for others. When I contacted her recently she told me, 'My Christian faith has been the engine of everything I do, including the forgiveness to the killers, and my love for everyone. I still learn about my journey from the time I begged the killers not to murder me, and then I had nothing, and my future was unclear. However, I went back to school and developed my career successfully, and I believe that anyone can be lifted up from vulnerability and become a successful person. My calling and responsibility is to be the hands and feet of my Lord and to reach out to the people who need to see his love.'

These home thoughts from abroad still contain a strong message for all of us, but it was a special outsider who came to our shores many centuries ago to change the course of Irish Church history, and who remains one of my all-time heroes.

15

The Footsteps of Patrick and Beyond

'I am Patrick, a sinner, most unlearned, the least of all the faithful, and utterly despised.'

Nearly all authors, and certainly all journalists, aspire to writing a compelling first sentence in their books or articles, and few introductions could be more compelling than this first sentence of St Patrick's autobiography, the *Confessio*, as quoted above.

In rudimentary Latin he writes in his *Confessio*, 'I was like a stone lying in the deep mire – and he that is mighty came in his mercy and lifted me up, and raised me aloft … my spirit was so moved so that in a single day I would say as many as a hundred prayers and almost as many in the night, and even when I was staying in the woods and on the mountains, and I used to get up for prayer before daylight, through snow, through frost, through rain, and I felt no harm, and there was no sloth in me – as I now see, because the spirit within me was then fervent.'[49]

It is hard not to be attracted to such a humble and spiritual human being as St Patrick. He was a slave and an enforced immigrant to Ireland who escaped after a vision but later returned voluntarily to bring the message of Christianity to the island. He was not the first missionary to do so; history records that Palladius came before him, but Patrick later caught the public imagination. He was an ordinary yet extraordinary human being, and was deservedly elevated to the sainthood. As the distinguished twentieth-century Irish diplomat and critical Patrician scholar

D. A. Binchy noted, 'The moral and spiritual greatness of the man shines through every stumbling sentence of his "rustic" Latin.'

From an early age I was attracted to St Patrick, though I cannot explain why. As a young Presbyterian I was sad that our church in Bessbrook did not mark St Patrick's Day with a service. It was left to the Catholics and the Anglicans to do so, though some fundamental Protestants dismissed the Anglicans sweepingly as 'half-Catholic' anyway. There was also a feeling in some quarters that Patrick was a 'Catholic saint'. It was only later that I had the opportunity to write about our patron saint in a book commissioned by Armagh Council to mark the new millennium, *St Patrick's City – the Story of Armagh*. The city clerk and chief executive Dessie Mitchell wisely persuaded the council that the money would be better spent on such an historic publication than on a fifteen-minute fireworks display on New Year's Eve.

The symbol of two of the citadels of Western Christendom existing apart for so many centuries is clearly seen in the city of Armagh itself, where the Protestant and Catholic cathedrals are situated on hills facing each other across a valley. For many decades there was little or no contact between two main denominations, but in more recent years there has been impressive cooperation between the respective primates, and with the heads of the other Churches. The days are gone when a Catholic primate made extremely rude comments publicly about the Orange Order, which were answered firmly by the Order, though not in quite the same tone.

The example of St Patrick has not only inspired but has also helped to soften the divisions, and, as the late Derick Bingham, a well-known Protestant evangelist, wrote of Patrick at the turn of the twenty-first century, 'Here is a faith-life for a new millennium in Ireland or anywhere else, that is incomparable. What Patrick brought is accessible to all.'[50] Bingham also referred to the popular and deeply spiritual hymn known as 'St Patrick's Breastplate', about which I also wrote a short book. The hymn, with words by Cecil Frances Alexander, the wife of a former archbishop of Armagh, and musical setting by Dublin-born Sir Charles Villiers Stanford, is regularly performed at Anglican services, though some non-Anglicans may feel irreverently that 'It does go on a bit'.

Shortly after completing my book on St Patrick, which was written shortly after I left my then full-time post as Head of Information at Queen's University to pursue a freelance writing career, I was approached by the *Belfast Telegraph* to fill the post of Religion Correspondent. It was an offer I couldn't refuse, as I had always had an interest in the subject, and this appointment marked yet another unexpected twist in my professional career.

As far back as the mid-1970s I had applied for the vacant post of Religion Correspondent with the *Irish Times*. Again, I find it difficult to explain why I did so, but by that stage I was becoming restless and was also drained by covering so much of the Troubles for the *Belfast Telegraph* and other publications, and I felt that I needed a change. The *Irish Times* editor Fergus Pyle, with whom I had worked when he was their Belfast correspondent, took me to lunch in Dublin. That was on the same day that I received a letter from Christian Aid offering me the opportunity to report on their work in the developing world.

Not long afterwards I was told that I did not get the *Irish Times* post, so it was an obvious move to accept the Christian Aid offer. Many years later I met a former news editor of the *Irish Times* who told me that I had missed the Religion Correspondent job by 'the skin of my teeth'. This made me wonder what I would have done if the *Irish Times* had offered me the job. It was only recently that I learned from 'an impeccable source', as we journalists say, that people at the highest level in the paper had asked themselves if this was the right time to appoint a Northern Ireland journalist from a Presbyterian background to fulfil the key post of Religion Correspondent of the *Irish Times*. This may have seemed to some a narrow and untypical *Irish Times* judgement, but it did not surprise me. On reflection I would have found it difficult to work my way in to a world where the Catholic Church was still so powerful in the Irish Republic and where so many of the child-sex abuse scandals had yet to be exposed. There was also the complication of perhaps having to move from Belfast to Dublin with my wife and school-aged children, so it was the right decision to accept the offer from Christian Aid.

Then, some thirty years later, I was given the surprise offer of the post of Religion Correspondent of the *Telegraph*. Not for the first time I asked myself if this was just a coincidence or if there was a hidden pattern to my career that I was unable or unwilling to recognise.

I settled into the *Telegraph* job quite quickly, and it gave me a fascinating insight into the life and work of the different Churches. As well as filing news stories and feature articles I wrote a hard-hitting weekly comment column, which often drew the wrath of the Churches as well as praise from some of the people who agreed with me. During this period I attended nearly all the annual church meetings, and I often told friends that the places where I least found God was at these synods and general assemblies. This was because of the political-religious grandstanding of a minority who used these ecclesiastical gatherings as a platform for their prejudices, sometimes unnoticed by the other delegates who were selflessly devoting their time and energy to the work of the Lord.

My work made me realise the loneliness of many church leaders and clerics who had to live with the realities of running a church and a congregation despite the flaws of human nature, including their own. Despite these drawbacks there was much evidence of genuine Christian service and love for others, which is often forgotten by the critics of the Churches, who choose to look only for flaws, of which there were, and are, many.

There was also more than a little dark humour in covering church affairs. On one occasion a reporter from another newspaper and I were interviewing a man who had been nominated for a senior role in his Church, which wanted some publicity for the appointment. He proved to be singularly lacking in any quotes that would help us to write a newsy report, so in desperation I asked him, 'Do you approve of same-sex relationships?' He replied, 'Yes', and we suddenly pricked up our ears. However, he then startled us by saying, 'When I was in theological college I was taught that when a couple were making love, the Holy Spirit left the room.' My journalistic colleague and I looked at each other, both wondering what headline a sub-editor would write on such a story. However, we decided to be merciful and ignore what the man had said. It was probably his first ever media interview, and he may have misheard the question.

There were many stories of cross-community help in times of trouble. In August 2002 Whitehouse Presbyterian Church near Belfast (my own church) was very badly damaged in a fire started by militant Republicans. Allegedly in reprisal for the attack on the church, loyalist paramilitaries petrol-bombed a home in a nearby Catholic housing estate later that day. Shortly afterwards the minister from Whitehouse, the Reverend Dr Liz Hughes, and May Jamison, an elder, visited the family to show the support of their Protestant neighbours.

At the next evening service, which had to be held in the church hall, because the main building was so badly damaged, the Catholic family came down with a jar of coins and notes that the grandchildren had collected from all round the neighbours to show their sympathy and to help with the church's rebuilding fund. The Presbyterian congregation was very moved by this, and that evening, in the words of Dr Hughes, 'There was hardly a dry eye in the Hall.'

Dr Hughes also told me, 'The extraordinary thing was that from the morning of the bomb explosion when the building was still smouldering, the whole community, including people from all walks of life, began to rally around. No matter who came to the site, we kept repeating to each other, 'The church is not the building, it is the people.' Our five neighbouring Catholic churches held a collection for us and presented us with a cheque for just under £10,000. Ironically, we had collected money for the nearby St Bernard's Catholic Church, which had been burned to the ground one year previously, and just a year later we were to receive that gift ten times over. It was wonderful how all the neighbouring churches came to our support.'

Those were terrible times. On another occasion a young postman had been murdered in an area not far from Whitehouse Church simply because he was a Catholic, and the story received widespread publicity. In an act of further sectarian hatred the headstone on his grave was desecrated. A Presbyterian elder read the story and sent £1,000 to the local Catholic priest, with the request to give it to the family to erect a new headstone. When they had done so, there were funds left over, and they gave the money back to the priest who then handed it over to Whitehouse Church for their rebuilding fund.

After talking with the Reverend Hughes I decided not to file the story because there was also the possibility that it might encourage the killers to return and to vandalise the new headstone. So it was never written or published. I am sure that I was not the first journalist or editor, then or since, to make such a decision.

No doubt there were many other unpublished stories like this from all across Northern Ireland during the Troubles. It underlines my point that despite the prevailing headlines there was always an innate decency among the vast majority from both main communities, who constantly gave support and comfort to each other across the religious divides. It was a continuing tragedy that there was not enough awareness or desire to turn this cross-community outreach into a lasting peaceful political settlement.

My role as Religion Correspondent also gave me the opportunity to cover a number of major stories, including the funeral of Pope John II in April 2005. I had also covered his visit to Ireland in the autumn of 1979. It was the first papal visit to Ireland and received massive publicity. I reported on the Pope's visit to Knock, and I was only a few feet from him as he made his way out of the packed basilica. I was once again aware of the loneliness of a human being in such a high-profile position. As Pope John Paul II slowly passed me by, I saw a female steward drop to her knees while he held out his hand to allow her to kiss the papal ring. It was as if she had seen the figure of Christ himself.

That afternoon the Pope gave a long homily while thousands of people stood outside in the fields during the rain. They included me, as the hair-shirt Presbyterian doing his duty briefly, while the rest of the press pack sheltered in the warmth of the church. I was also amused by the fact that we had to file our copy from confessional boxes improvised to create telephone booths, and later on I smiled when I heard the band of the Garda Síochána (the Irish police force) playing the Orange Order's song, 'The Sash My Father Wore'. It had been a long day but they had not lost their sense of humour.

So there was a certain symmetry in my visit to Rome to report on John Paul II's funeral, two days before it took place. Shortly after my arrival I walked among the huge crowds towards St Peter's Square. I was wearing a large dark overcoat and hat with a red scarf which, I hoped, might give me the authority of a cardinal, because I did not have a Vatican press pass. Instead I was using a press pass for President Reagan's visit to Ballyporeen in Ireland several years previously, but miraculously it worked. A seasoned reporter might be well intentioned but he or she also needs to be streetwise on occasions.

I made my way into St Peter's Square, to the background sound of readings from Romans of which the Reverend Ian Paisley himself would have approved, and eventually into the basilica itself, where I stood only a few feet from the Pope, lying in state. It was the exact spot where President Bill Clinton, Condoleezza Rice and President George W. Bush had stood only hours previously.

I was in St Peter's Square again on the day of the funeral among many thousands of people who had come to pay their last respects. I was standing among young Eastern Europeans when I felt a strong push on my back from a woman with a large camera and a set of steps over her shoulder. I thought she was Polish and I was trying to explain to her that she could not get through – whereupon she said, 'I know who you are. You're Alf McCreary! I'm from the *Belfast Newsletter*.' It was one of those moments when life was stranger than fiction.

The funeral service continued movingly while I filed my copy with my then very basic mobile phone. At the end, the pall-bearers turned the coffin one last time, and beside me a nun with a white scarf waved and shouted passionately, 'Adieu, Papa, Adieu.' I marvelled how she and so many thousands of other young people had such an affection for this conservative and elderly pope, but I was also aware that as well as having enormous charisma, John Paul II had also drawn deeply from the most enduring and inspiring elements of the Christian faith. Reporting on his funeral was one of the highlights of my career. I was aware that I was part of history in the making and I was again reminded of the continuing importance of the Christian faith to so many people, despite the encroachment of secularism.

My work as Religion Correspondent for the *Belfast Telegraph* has given me a wide perspective of faith in practice, with all its virtues and setbacks. I admire those people who devote their lives to the ministry and I respect people from all backgrounds who earnestly try to follow the Christian example. I disagree with some aspects of what they believe, but I do not do so judgementally. They are entitled to their own opinions and if people are happier and lead better lives because of their faith, so be it. I find that very impressive. What I cannot abide, however, are those who are quick to tell you that you are wrong, and that only they have the ear of the Almighty. Sadly, these attitudes have been all too prevalent in Northern Ireland, and other parts of our island. We could all learn from our St Patrick, who humbly and clearly showed us a better way a very long time ago.

16

Patrick, Paisley and the Pope

One of the best-known supporters of St Patrick was the Reverend Dr Ian Paisley, who dominated Northern Ireland politics for decades but who also demonstrated that he was one of the most unlikely people qualified to follow the example of the patron saint of Ireland. However, this was all part of the complexity of Ian Paisley, who created so many headlines throughout his career, but whose journey of 'keeping the faith' often showed little of the breadth and compassion of the Gospel teaching. That said, however, he seemed oblivious to the contradiction between his Christian beliefs and many of his actions, and he continually heaped praise on St Patrick.

On 7 February 2000 the Northern Ireland Assembly at Stormont debated a motion that St Patrick's Day should become a public holiday. It led to a lively exchange of views, during which Dr Paisley told the members, 'I, like all other right-thinking people in Ulster, regret the sectarian and political label that has been put on St Patrick. Professor John Barkley was a well-known historian and a leader in the Irish Presbyterian Church, who wrote a book in which he asked the question "Was the early Irish Church subject to Rome?" He answered "No." The Independence of the early Irish Church is one of the most indisputable facts in history.'

Paisley was about to launch into a longer explanation, when his mobile phone rang. He 'humbly' apologised to the House because mobile phones were banned in the Chamber. Then another member suggested to Dr Paisley, 'Perhaps it is St Patrick on the line?' to laughter all round.

As the debate continued, Dr Paisley said, 'I refuse to hand St Patrick over to the Roman Catholic Church and the embrace of the Pope, or to the IRA or Nationalists. He is a figure to be honoured and remembered. In his works – the *Confession*, the Epistle and the Hymn – one finds set forth the simple Gospel of Jesus Christ. "God so loved the world, that he gave his only begotten son, that whosoever believeth in Him should not perish, but have everlasting life." We should honour St Patrick and have a public holiday declared by the Secretary of State.'[51]

This debate illustrated the ability of Ian Paisley to use arguments to suit himself. He quoted the Reverend John Barkley as an historian and 'a leader in the Irish Presbyterian Church', yet it was the same Irish Presbyterian Church that Paisley spent so much of his career trying to undermine.

Paisley had a continually high profile, and in 2006 a leading academic from the Ulster Museum, the archaeologist Dr Richard Warner, gave a lecture on 'St Patrick, the Man and the Myth'. Afterwards, answering questions, he said, 'From my reading of St Patrick's writings and what I observe about Dr Paisley, both had something in common, including very great strength of purpose and an unshakeable belief in the Word of God. I can almost hear Ian Paisley's voice coming through when I read the writings of Patrick. There is one major difference, however. Dr Paisley has a good sense of humour, something which Patrick did not possess.'[52]

In an article in the *Irish Times* three years later, Paisley described St Patrick as 'a very humble man who did not put any sugar on the lollipop of his deeply held Christian belief. Patrick knew his Bible and he must have come from a family which taught him the Scriptures. Patrick has been hijacked by the Roman Catholic Church and made to be something he wasn't.'[53]

Given his respect for St Patrick, it seems strange that Paisley seemed not to grasp the message of reconciliation and of loving one's neighbour that lies at the heart of the Gospel, and he showed a lifelong and vitriolic hatred of Roman Catholicism.

He regularly referred to popes as 'Old Red Socks', a cheap jibe which invariably was greeted with laughter by his followers. He also voiced strong objections to the visit of Pope John Paul II to Ireland in 1979. At a plenary session of the European Parliament in Strasbourg in October 1988, which was being addressed by John Paul II, Ian Paisley denounced him as an 'anti-Christ' and was removed protesting from the chamber.

This was a calculated move to ensure that his profile remained high, and to underline that his opposition to the papacy remained undiminished. Years later he travelled to Edinburgh to protest the UK visit of Pope Benedict, and in 2004, when Cardinal Seán Brady was invited to the Presbyterian General Assembly by the incoming moderator, the Right Reverend Kenneth Newell, a group of Free Presbyterian ministers formed a grim-faced circle of protestors outside the building. Fortunately the Presbyterians in Church House gave the cardinal a polite welcome.

It is important to point out, however, that while Paisley had a deep hatred of Roman Catholicism, he was not necessarily hostile to individual Catholics. A number of his Catholic constituents in North Antrim praised his support as their MP. This was part of the astuteness of Paisley, who was keen to counter any allegations that he was hostile to individual Catholics, in contrast to his virulent opposition to Catholicism.

Ian Paisley's barn-storming style and hostility towards militant Republicanism had an effect on many Loyalists, who fiercely opposed Republican paramilitary groups, including the Provisional IRA. A large number of those who took up arms paid the price and served long prison sentences, and some expressed regret about ever having listened to the fiery rhetoric of the street preacher.

Over the years Paisley organised a large number of protest rallies, including the march in 1966 through a Catholic area of Cromac

Street on his way to Church House in the centre of Belfast, where verbal abuse was hurled at the official party attending the opening night of the General Assembly (see Chapter 6). The Cromac Street confrontation with Catholic youths led to rioting. Ian Paisley and six others were charged with unlawful assembly and were convicted, fined and bound over to keep the peace for two years. As historian Jonathan Bardon notes, 'Paisley refused to enter into the bail bond and on 20 July he was lodged in Crumlin Road gaol. The following weekend the police failed to quell rioting Protestants in the Shankill Road with baton charges, and water cannon had to be brought in to stop the looting of Catholic-owned public houses.'[54] Not surprisingly Paisley's imprisonment helped to sustain his claim as a 'martyr' for the cause of Protestantism. Two years later Paisley and an associate, Major Ronald Bunting, were jailed for six weeks for unlawful assembly after they organised an illegal counter-demonstration in opposition to a scheduled civil rights march in Armagh.[55]

Paisley organised numerous other rallies and also led some of his supporters in the manner of the fabled Grand Old Duke of York, who marched his men to the top of the hill and then marched them down again. Some of these protests were very serious, while others had dimensions of melodrama and farce, but they helped to underline the alarming possibility that there were Loyalist militias and other shadowy groups ready to defend Protestant interests by whatever means necessary. Was this threat of disorder just another clever ploy of Paisley's to heap more political pressure on the British establishment, which was desperately trying to find a solution to the endlessly intractable Ulster deadlock, or was it something else? All of this was part of the enigma that was Ian Paisley.

Indisputably, however, Ian Paisley made his greatest impact through politics. He built a powerful grass-roots organisation, which led to the formation in 1964 of the Protestant Unionist Party, the forerunner of his Democratic Unionist Party, which he established in 1971. By 2005 it had eclipsed the Official Unionist

Party, which had dominated politics in the North of Ireland for the previous century.

It is difficult to think of another figure who could have taken his place to the same extent, and who could have stirred up so much trouble. Ian Paisley recognised the deep fears of grass-roots Unionists and gave them a voice. In doing so he eventually became the most powerful Protestant political leader in Northern Ireland.

He led the DUP from 1971 until 2008, he was the Westminster Unionist MP for North Antrim from 1970 until 2010, a Member of the European Parliament from 1979 until 2004, a member of the Legislative Assembly for North Antrim from 1998–2011, and a life peer from 2010 until his death in 2014. His greatest early success was his victory over former Northern Ireland Prime Minister Captain Terence O'Neil in 1970, when he secured the Bannside seat in the Northern Ireland parliament. He was the rabble-rousing street preacher who came of age politically and became a force to be reckoned with for decades to come.

His upward political trajectory was propelled by his religious fundamentalism and his hard-line unionism, which brooked no rivals. He helped to destroy successive Unionist leaders who showed any signs of liberalism, he opposed the Sunningdale Agreement of 1973, which attempted to set up a power-sharing government of nationalists and unionists, he campaigned against the Anglo-Irish Agreement, and he strongly opposed the Good Friday Agreement of 1998, widely hailed as a breakthrough towards a lasting settlement in Northern Ireland.

It is therefore hard to exaggerate the sense of political shock in Belfast, London and Dublin when he led his Democratic Unionist Party to share power with Sinn Féin and other parties at Stormont in 2007. Paisley became First Minister, and the former Provisional IRA leader Martin McGuinness became the Deputy First Minister. These former political enemies got on so well together that they were nicknamed the 'Chuckle Brothers', but it was a tragedy that Paisley achieved power so late in his life when his health was deteriorating, and McGuinness died relatively young from a heart complaint. If both men had come together a decade or more earlier, the success of power-sharing might have been more secure than it was subsequently, with long absences by the DUP and Sinn Féin from Stormont, and the sporadic breakdowns in power-sharing.

However, the major political question is 'Why did Ian Paisley decide to share power with Sinn Féin?' Was it the pragmatism of a man who had such a huge ego that he founded his own Free Presbyterian Church, his own newspaper, the *Protestant Telegraph*, and his own Democratic Unionist Party, and had always craved the top job? Or did he choose to share power from a higher spiritual motive?

I am still not sure about the answer, even though I was brought very close to Paisley physically when I reported his resignation as moderator of his Free Presbyterian Church. This meeting took place on a winter's night in the Dungannon Free Presbyterian Church when I waited in the chill rain with the press corps to try to find out what was happening. Security was tight, and every time I tried to find a chink of light or a snippet of news escaping from the building I was followed by a beady-eyed Paisley-ite warning me off. I should add, however, that the ladies in the church hall showed a commendable Christian spirit by fortifying us with tea and excellent sandwiches.

Shortly after 9.30 pm, and well in time for the 10 o'clock BBC News bulletins, Paisley and a senior colleague emerged from the church to announce that he was no longer the moderator. He did not say that he had been sacked, but that is what it amounted to. Paisley had proved unable to continue managing his political and religious fundamentalism in tandem, and his political profile and his power-sharing with Sinn Féin proved too much for a large proportion of his church members.

Paisley was no doubt deeply hurt and disappointed by the outcome after serving for fifty-eight years as moderator, but he did not show it as he indulged in knockabout banter with the members of the press outside the church. I was standing almost shoulder to shoulder and slightly behind him in my all-weather gear and I could see clearly the interplay that was going on. Paisley was enjoying his jousting with the media, and they with him. One reporter shouted, 'Will you miss us, Dr Paisley?' He replied, 'Not at all, sir. I will not have any editor telling Ian Paisley what to do. If there are any more impertinent questions from you I will box your ears.'

However, there was a serious note when one reporter asked him, 'Why did you share power with Sinn Féin?' Instead of firing back a quick sound bite, Paisley gave a slow, thoughtful explanation. This seemed to me to be based on the spiritual dimension of a man who had been through a serious illness, and who realised that his time for doing good might be limited. I gave him the benefit of the doubt and I thought that maybe he genuinely wanted the best for everyone in Northern Ireland, and that his sharing of power was not just an ego trip.

Later on I became unsure about that. Many people would claim that Ian Paisley was a supreme egotist, and that his climb up the greasy pole to become first minister was the result of intense political ambition that was clothed in religious posturing.

The author William Brown, who knew Paisley well from an early age as an acquaintance of his own evangelical preacher father, described Paisley as 'a Jekyll and Hyde – as a charismatic character, yet often a frighteningly forbidding one. This latter characterisation would develop out of my growing disenchantment with his extreme species of religious politics – an unhealthy conjunction. The more I came to know him, the stronger this increased to the point where I saw him as the most dangerous man in Northern Ireland.'[56]

William Brown's insightful book is tellingly titled *Ian Paisley as I Knew Him – Charismatic, Chameleon or Charlatan?* Certainly, Paisley may have often demonstrated all three qualities, and a great many more. The former senior civil servant Maurice Hayes believed that there were 'at least six Ian Paisleys'.

Nevertheless, he was a remarkable character, with extraordinary talents as well as serious flaws. Near the end of his life I met him at a function in Belfast City Hall, when I was introduced by the Sinn Féin Lord Mayor Máirtín Ó Muilleoir. He was benign and good-humoured, which surprised me, given the hostility there had been in earlier days between the *Belfast Telegraph* and Paisley himself. He asked me my age, and when I told him, he answered with pride, 'I am older than you.' Then he asked, 'What do you think will be the future in Ireland?' I replied, 'It's me should be asking you that!' He said, 'Both parts of the island will prosper, but separately.'

He seemed content in his old age, despite his disappointment and a certain bitterness about having to resign as the Free Presbyterian Moderator, and as leader of the Democratic Unionist Party. Self-made men like Paisley do not give up power lightly, as they relinquish office and move into the wilderness.

Some apologists for Paisley point out that his personal views were also those of a large number of fundamental evangelical Protestants and hard-line Unionists in Northern Ireland, and that he was an extremely complex man. However, I do not agree with that interpretation of Paisley and his contribution to the history of Northern Ireland. Despite his charm, eloquence, humour and other admirable qualities, and not least as a family man, I still believe that Ian Paisley had much for which to answer. To his credit he made power sharing possible, thus decreasing the horrendous level of violence that had disfigured Northern Ireland for so long, but he was also the man who destroyed every attempt at a political settlement years before the emergence of the Provisional IRA and assorted Loyalist paramilitary violence. That is something that I cannot overlook. In my journey of 'keeping the faith' I have encountered few such human beings who claimed devotion to Christianity, but who also created so much misery and inspired so much sectarianism as the late Ian Richard Kyle Paisley, the evangelist and political activist.

One of my abiding memories of Paisley was his last sermon in his packed Martyrs Memorial Church in Belfast to which the press had been invited. It was an offer I could not refuse; I never imagined that I would be invited to Paisley's church. His final fundamentalist Protestant sermon was exactly the same as the one that he had preached at the start of his ministry, and I felt sad that he had moved 'not an inch' in his theology, despite moving miles in his political career by sharing power with the old enemy, Sinn Féin, and with a former Provisional IRA leader.

Prior to the sermon there was a reading from the Bible and a gentle lady in a beret who was sitting beside me asked nicely if I would like to share her copy of the New Testament with her. I did so gladly, but she did not notice that I was wearing red socks in solidarity with all the popes whom Paisley had verbally abused over the decades by calling them 'Old Red Socks'. Paisley would not have noticed me either, as I sat in the church he built, but I thought that in the presence of the great man himself, who had been virtually the 'Protestant' pope of Ulster in his heyday, it was the least that I could do as an 'unfree' mainstream Presbyterian to show my respect for the Vatican and for the Catholicism that Paisley had so despised all his life.

One of the great 'If onlys' of Northern Ireland's history is to ask what would have been achieved for good if Ian Paisley had used his enormous gifts in order to build bridges earlier in his career and not in his old age when it was much too late to try to do so. The people from all the communities in Northern Ireland deserved something much, much better, but they did not get it.

17

Keeping the Faith

One cold night in Armagh, I had time on my hands before reporting for the *Belfast Telegraph* on the return of the Catholic primate Seán Brady, who had just been made a cardinal in Rome. Armagh is the ecclesiastical capital of Ireland, but on a winter's evening it can be godforsaken. To while away the minutes I had a solitary meal in a local café, after which I set out for St Patrick's Cathedral on my way to welcome home the new cardinal.

I should say that I was wearing my long black coat, with a broad-brimmed hat and a bright red scarf. On my way past a pub the front door suddenly burst open, a generously imbibed customer was propelled forward and landed on his back on the pavement, right before my eyes. I peered down to see if he was all right, whereupon he focused a beady eye on me, and then burst into a loud and jolly exclamation, 'It's Dr Paisley, welcome to Armagh!'

Warmed with such a mistaken welcome, I hurried towards the cathedral and waited for the cardinal's procession to make its way up the hill. As it passed, he beckoned me to join him. We walked together for two or three minutes while Cardinal Brady, always a gentleman, thanked me for my coverage of his visit to Rome. When we had finished talking, I slipped back into the crowd, and then a young reporter with his notebook in hand stopped to talk to me. He said, 'Excuse me, sir, I noticed you talking to the cardinal a moment or two ago. Are you a Catholic bishop?' I replied, 'Young man I admire your initiative in asking me that question, but I am not a Catholic bishop. I am a press reporter, just like you!'

Privately, however, I was amused at being mistaken for Paisley and then for a Catholic bishop, and both on the same night in the space of an hour. Looking back it symbolised neatly the number of faith stories that I had covered for the *Belfast Telegraph* and other publications at home and abroad. These ranged broadly from Irish Catholicism to fundamental Protestant evangelism, though I often stress that for the major part of my earlier career I wrote about the Troubles rather than about church affairs.

My journey in this book has been for me a time of reflection, sometimes painful and at other times reassuring, and of trying to keep faith in the progression, or in some cases the regression, of my chosen profession, as well as my inner faith in things spiritual, and also in the goodness, and often otherwise, of human nature. The interaction between these two absorbing and continuing interests of my life is well expressed by what I regard to be one of the most important questions in history. That question was asked of Jesus Christ by Pontius Pilate, who knew that the figure standing before him was innocent, but that for political reasons and for his own career prospects and safety, he could not afford to free him. So when Christ said to Pilate, 'Everyone who belongs to the truth hears my voice', the governor asked him, with a sense of exasperation and perhaps of guilt at handing over an innocent man to his certain death, 'What is truth?' After that he told the Jewish accusers, 'I find no case against him' (John 18:37–38).

What is truth Indeed? In my early days when reporting the Troubles in Northern Ireland we journalists were often accused by people with fixed political views of not telling the truth. My standard reply was, 'You tell me your truth, and I will tell you mine.' That was a long time ago, but the challenge of 'What is truth?' remains. Nowadays, with the benefit of hindsight, I can reflect on how journalism has changed from my early days, with only the relatively limited news coverage by three daily newspapers in Belfast and a few daily reports on BBC Radio and Television, to today's virtual torrent of information and comment on almost every subject. As I recalled earlier in this book, my former editor Roy Lilley used to say to me that the best news coverage was on Sky TV, but only for fifteen minutes or so until the demands of the recent invention of 'rolling news' led to endless repeats of the same information over a twenty-four-hour period.

The sheer number and range of these reports have become in themselves a challenge to truth, depending on which newspaper you read or which television channel you watch. There are so many 'experts', who often present starkly different views on the same subject, and also 'influencers' and public relations 'gurus', who skilfully add or subtract an edge to or from the news that may be to their advantage. Therefore it is very difficult for ordinary people to make up their own minds about what is the 'truth'. Many years ago I was told by a Harvard lecturer at the influential Salzburg Seminar series in Austria that newspapers don't necessarily make people change their minds about anything, because they tend to read the newspapers and listen to the television and radio reports that confirm their own views.

The modern assault on truth is compounded by the exchanges on social media between millions of people who believe that their views do not have to take note of the true facts. This is strongly in contrast to my days as a young reporter when my editors drummed into me the importance of keeping to the facts and of writing a fair and balanced account of everything I reported. The situation is now so bad that many people claim that there is no harm in deliberately telling lies, even though in a court of law this avoidance or twisting of the truth is regarded as perjury, which carries a high penalty. Some of the blatant lies of political leaders in recent years have been deeply unsettling, particularly when many of these go unchallenged.

One of the greatest challenges to honest reporting and the search for truth has come from the deeply flawed Donald Trump, who has elevated the claim of 'fake news' to become the mantra of millions of people who immediately dismiss anything with which they do not agree. This has done untold harm to the responsible media and to editors and reporters the world over. One expects Russia, as one example of a dictatorship, to tell lies as a way of life, but it is disconcerting to hear people in high places within some of the free democratic societies of the West habitually telling lies as a matter of fact.

As if this is not bad enough, we now face the deeply worrying challenge from the onslaught of artificial intelligence, which has great potential for good or evil. Faced with all these burdens, the question from Pontius Pilate more than 2,000 years ago has a modern urgency which challenges all of us – what indeed is 'truth'?

After a career of nearly sixty years, I have not lost my faith in the honest young journalists who show great courage and ingenuity in trying to get to the truth. However, I do worry about the over-reporting of events and the trivialising of so much else, as well as the pervasive cult of celebrity, and the huge emphasis on sport, which has become the new religion. Far too many news outlets, in their desperation to attract and hold readers and viewers, give people too much of what they want and not enough of what they need to know. It is almost as if much of the modern media sets out to entertain readers and viewers, rather than inform them about serious things that will challenge and shape their lives.

I believe that I, and my contemporaries, have had the best of the last vestiges of written journalism on a mass scale, from the mid-sixties until recent times. I admire the young people who still want to join this tough though creatively rewarding profession, with its increasing financial and ethical challenges, and the possible demise of most of print journalism. I wish them well.

Some sixty years ago, I was told by the distinguished *Belfast Telegraph* journalist Cal McCrystal, who later became an outstanding reporter with the *Sunday Times*, 'You will never become rich from journalism, but it will make you a rich human being.' I listened carefully to his advice, but joined the *Belfast Telegraph* anyhow, and I discovered how right he was. Would I do it so eagerly again in the modern world of journalism? I probably would, but I would think very long and hard about it. However, I remain deeply grateful for the writing career I have been able to follow up to now, during which I reported on so many of the big stories during the Troubles for local, national and international outlets, as well as making extensive visits to so many different fascinating, challenged and sometimes dangerous parts of the developing world.

Sadly, however, one of my big professional disappointments is the lack of a permanent political settlement thus far in Northern Ireland, despite the efforts of the many people on all sides and from other countries who have worked so hard to build bridges between the two communities to help make peace a reality. In my earlier career in the *Belfast Telegraph* my colleagues and I poured our hearts and souls into helping to build bridges, and now I sometimes wonder if our efforts were totally in vain, though the culmination of the efforts of so many of us found expression in the aptly named Good Friday Agreement of 10 April 1998.

However, so much more remains to be done. At a Shared Island event in Dublin in October 2023 Tánaiste Mícheál Martin said, 'While there has been immense progress, clearly the vision of the Good Friday Agreement for a reconciliation of all communities and traditions has not yet been achieved.' He added that how to accommodate different national identities remained 'one of the great challenges of our time ... it is time to find ways to move our respective cultures and identities fully on from dichotomy and rivalry to symbiosis and respect.'[57] Looking back, I feel that I and my colleagues could not have done more to further that objective, and now I must leave it to a younger generation to take up the challenge with their own youthful energy and enthusiasm.

Afterword

My journey of keeping the faith in spiritual matters has been complex, but I have had the advantage of a writing career that has given me the opportunity to meet a very large number of people from different denominations and faiths. Many of these people have taught me something, and they have also challenged me to ask myself many questions about the essence of Christianity and other beliefs.

Certainly my idea of faith has developed from that of a five-year-old child who, like many others of his age in the mid-1940s, was taught that God was a dark, judgemental figure living above the clouds, with a black book in which he wrote down all our sins, for which we would have to pay a penalty. Equally, I am aware that church attendance nowadays is a personal choice, not necessarily obligatory, and that utterances from the pulpit have to be judged on their own merit rather than being accepted without question.

Of course I have heard many brilliant and inspiring sermons, but I have winced through lots that were eminently forgettable. Unfortunately, most churchgoers tend not to tell the preacher when they think the sermon was poor, and they complain only to each other. They really should do the preacher a favour and say what they really think. I recall a critical Northern Catholic friend satirising in despair a fictional but symbolic sermon in which his bishop spent most of his address criticising the local transportation plan, and then rounding it off with a biblical reassurance that 'God is love', which would have been a remarkable non sequitur by any standard.

The decline in church membership and attendance in recent years has been well-documented, and sometimes it is the details, rather than a table of the global statistics, that make me take a deep breath. My colleague Patsy McGarry, the former religion editor of the *Irish Times*, reported on 25 February 2023 that plans are being made in the Catholic Archdiocese of Dublin for the laity to play a much bigger role. He wrote, 'Though it was once unthinkable, it is just a matter of time before funerals are being conducted on a regular basis by lay people in the Archdiocese of Dublin and elsewhere in the State – as well as marriages and baptisms. Everything but the Mass and the blessing of the Sacraments, in fact.' On 4 April 2023 the London *Times* reported that 'for the first time in the Church of England's history more than a quarter of churches no longer hold a service every Sunday … because of exhausted priests, tired volunteers and financial struggles …', despite the fact that there was still a demand from worshippers for regular Sunday services.

Though these facts are depressing, they are part of the well-known wider story of the Churches in relative decline. However, it is harder to pin down the reasons for this lack of interest. They include the relentless march of the secular society, the fact that many people no longer feel that they need God and are searching elsewhere on their spiritual journey, the reality that the Churches are answering many of the questions that people are not asking, as well as the scandal of clerical child sex abuse, and many other ecclesiastical wrongs and abuses over many decades, the poor track record of the Church when it has tried to dictate to and to talk down to people, and the common view among the general public that the Church is no longer relevant to much of daily life. Added to this is the effect of the recent Covid-19 pandemic, which closed churches, and has led to many people returning to worship only now and again instead of every Sunday.

So many questions are still unanswered. Is spirituality replacing traditional organised religion? Are we facing a global struggle between 'good and evil', however old-fashioned that seems? Are enough people recognising the radicalism in the Gospels, and is there is more to Christianity than saving their souls? How will the Church deal with the massive challenges posed by climate change and artificial intelligence?

There is also the question of church vestments, liturgy and language, which reassure many believers but which put others off. I have often made the point that while churchgoers might feel estranged if they entered a bookmaker's premises, the opposite also applies to those who are regular visitors to the bookies, who would feel equally strange if they entered a church.

While elaborate clerical vestments are a problem for some people, who think that they look ridiculous in the modern age, the lack of robes in many of the evangelical Protestant Churches creates another problem. The intention may be to show that the minister is 'one of us', but that does not impress me, because the clergy are ordained to fill a special position in leadership and teaching, and in that sense they are definitely not 'one of us'.

There is also the challenge of transmitting the Christian faith itself. I often wonder if the Churches realise that they are trying to pass on a message that seems utterly incredible in the modern world – namely that if someone runs off with your wife or husband or partner you must forgive him or her, and if someone thumps you, it is right to turn the other cheek; and when you die you don't really die, because you will be judged on your life here on earth, and the outcome will determine whether you spend the rest of eternity in heaven or hell. There was a time when millions of people accepted that message largely without question, but not any more.

For several years I have featured a regular online full-page interview in the *Belfast Telegraph* in a series titled 'What I Believe'. I am grateful that so many people are willing to reveal their inner thoughts so lucidly, and I notice that there are two broad categories. There are those who claim that they are 'saved' or 'born again', often from an early age, and who go through life with total faith and without questioning Christianity and their Christian commitment. However, there are others, with whom I empathise, who struggle at times with their faith, but who never give up. One of the recurring themes in the interviews is the hurt that the Churches have caused. One of the questions I always ask is, 'Why are so many people turning their backs on organised religion?' One clerical respondent replied recently, 'Many don't see it as relevant; they don't want to be told what to do, and they have been hurt by those who feel that their view is the only view which counts.' Recently I have widened my list of interviewees to include people of other faiths or none at all, and this is a significant sign of the times.

The major challenge facing the Churches today is to make the Christian message meaningful and inspiring, but not to allow themselves to become places only for happy-clappy, feel-good worship, while at the same time fudging the reality that Christianity demands hard choices, as well as personal and collective discipline and remarkable unselfishness. These qualities are conspicuous by their absence in the modern world. I have long treasured the observation by G. K. Chesterton that 'the Christian ideal has not been tried and found wanting. It has been found difficult and left untried. He who begins by loving Christianity better than Truth will proceed by loving his own sect or church better than Christianity, and end by loving himself better than all.'[58]

Some people have intellectual difficulties accepting faith and the concept of spirituality, and I found this particularly so when working at Queen's University for more than fourteen years, despite the work of the Protestant and Catholic chaplaincies, which did such good work in reaching out to students – just as the Presbyterian Reverend Ray Davey did in the sixties when I was a student at the university, to my great benefit then and in the longer term.

As Information Director at Queen's over thirty years later I remember interviewing an academic who had a special interest in religion, and when I asked him if he himself had a faith, he looked at me rather scornfully. I did not mind that, because by that time I was mature enough not to worry about what academics thought.

I realised that very many of them covered their deep insecurities with a thick or thin layer of scholarly arrogance.

Some months later I helped to draft a funeral oration for that same, likeable man, who had tragically taken his own life. It was a humanist funeral, and I remember asking the Vice-Chancellor Sir Gordon Beveridge if we might get away with at least one mention of God in his address.

I also remember my first vice-chancellor boss Sir Peter Froggatt telling me on my first day in the job, 'You will be working with some very smart people, but you will find that many of them are prone to outsmarting themselves.' There was a time when I frequently exchanged views with atheist friends and acquaintances but I found that most of them were just as fixed in their atheism as the most conservative Christian evangelicals. So I ended up by saying, 'If you are right and there is no God, neither of us need to worry about the future; but if I am right about the existence of an afterlife, you will soon find out once you pass on!'

It was Belfast's own incisive Christian writer C. S. Lewis who typically cut to the heart of this debate when he wrote in his book *Mere Christianity*, 'Either this man [Jesus] was, and is, the Son of God, or else a madman or something worse. You can shut him up for a fool, you can spit at him and kill him as a demon, or you can fall at his feet and call him Lord and God, but let us not come with any patronising nonsense about his being a great human teacher. He has not left that open to us. He did not intend to.'[59] I have never thought that Christ Jesus was either a fool or a madman.

Despite my many reservations, like those of others, about organised religion, I still respect the Churches and particularly those men and women who devote their lives to trying to present the best of the Christian faith. It is an often lonely and difficult calling, and the clergy, like the Churches, are often overlooked for the good they do. However, before I become too rosy-eyed, I should record that two of the nastiest comments I received in my career came from clerics, including a Church of England bishop. After our bruising public encounter, a helpful lady said to me, 'That was very nasty, but I suppose a weren't hurt. You are a journalist, after all!' I replied, 'Thanks for your kind comment, but in fact I *was* hurt. Journalists are human beings too. We also bleed on occasions, but generally we try not to show it.'

On the positive side, one of the most impressive examples of the Church speaking strongly to violence and power was at the tribute service for Lyra McKee, the courageous and visionary young journalist who was fatally wounded during disturbances involving dissident Republicans in the Creggan area of Derry/Londonderry on 18 April 2019, when shots were fired at the police.

The service in St Anne's Cathedral in Belfast, which I reported for my newspaper, was attended by the major leading politicians from London, Dublin and Belfast. They sat in a row in front of a large group of the ordinary people who filled the cathedral. The eloquent tribute to Lyra was delivered powerfully by Father Martin Magill, one of her many friends, and a copy of his speech was handed out to the media in advance. I noted one brief section that went straight to the heart of the matter. Father Magill said, slowly and clearly, 'Many of us will be praying that Lyra's death in its own way will not have been in vain and will contribute in some way to building peace here. Since Thursday night we have seen the coming together of many people in various places, and the unifying of the community against violence. I commend our political leaders for standing together in Creggan on Good Friday.'

Then he added these words, 'I am, however, left with a question. Why in God's name does it take the death of a twenty-nine-year-old woman with her whole life in front of her to get us to this point?' Even before he had finished, the large congregation rose spontaneously to its feet amid loud and sustained applause.

The people were well ahead of the assembled politicians at the front, who rose to their feet all-too slowly. This reinforced my long-held view that the ordinary people are so often ahead of the politicians, but what depresses me is the way in which the voters seem to elect the same old faces into positions where in Northern Ireland they have been totally unable so far to agree on a lasting political settlement. Nevertheless, so long as the Church continues to speak to violence and power with the radical clarity of Father McGill on that memorable occasion it will continue to play a vital and pivotal role in keeping the faith.

However, I have also noticed some reassuring comments in the British press recently which suggest that the lack of morality in much of public life and concern about global issues is not just the concern of the Churches. Following the results of a survey, which claimed that about three-quarters of Church of England clergy believe that the UK could no longer be described as a Christian country, the *Sunday Times* published this headline to a column by the highly perceptive writer Rod Liddle in its edition of 3 September 2023: 'Great, we banished Christianity. Now we're stuck in a moral wilderness'. Mr Liddle wrote, 'The retreat of Christianity in our country – or more properly our collective retreat from it – has enormously diminished us, both as individuals and as a society. The strictures of the old Church may have been confining and rudimentary by our modern standards, but they provided a template by which we could live decent lives in a cohesive society.' He also referred to the crucial 'notion that we are not alone, that we are being watched and judged from above. Without it we subside naturally into narcissism, amorality and that most modern of phrases never far from our lips when we have done something venal, stupid or selfish "Don't judge me!"'

Only a few weeks later Matthew Syed, another distinguished *Sunday Times* columnist, writing in its 22 October 2023 edition, claimed that the 'rising axis' of China, Iran, North Korea and Russia is 'more powerful than Nazi Germany, more strategically threatening than the Soviet Union.' He added, 'It is time to wake up and smell the danger … this is a battle between good and evil, just as it was in 1939, and just as it was in the Cold War. Unless we see this, and see it clearly, we will not be able to muster either the resolve or clarity to win. And win we must.'

On 20 July 2023 the London *Times* ran a headline on a column by James Marriott: 'We're fiddling with trivia as the world burns.'

It is encouraging to read these sentiments in the hope that many others will share them, and to note that there are also prophetic voices as well as those in the Churches – as the theologian Paul Tillich predicted in the 1950s.

Currently the Churches in the West are declining in number, but I believe that they can still play an important role in our national life, and in the lives of many millions of individuals around the globe, including in the developing world, where church membership is burgeoning. Some of the best values of Christianity have established the basis for the moral standards of our national life, and we ignore these teachings at our peril. The Churches, with all their strengths, and despite their many human faults, can and will continue to provide challenge and comfort with the guidance of the Holy Spirit, but in a way that is not always clear to us. Christianity has survived more than two millennia of major upheavals, as well as intellectual challenges and, in many eras, periods of prolonged indifference. I believe that if it keeps pace with the times and does not compromise on its core teachings – which will be no mean feat – it will continue to 'keep the faith' and transform people who are searching for comfort, as well as inspiration, and a meaning to their lives.

I also firmly believe that Christianity will continue to comfort the afflicted and to afflict the comfortable, and therein lies the hope for all of us. A future without a journey of faith, hope and spirituality at its best is to me unthinkable. So, despite all my shortcomings, I still live in hope both for here and for hereafter. I continue to be strengthened by the examples of those people named in this book, and by many others who have inspired me by demonstrating their strong Christian faith in times of great loss and distress, as well as the agnostics and those of different faiths or none who have shown qualities that are also inspiring and life-affirming.

I try not to judge people according to what they say they believe or what church they attend, but primarily on the kind of lives they lead. During many years of reporting I had to write about far too many harrowing scenes during the Troubles and also about the widespread deprivation and suffering in the developing world. However, I was also often inspired by the courage, resilience and generosity of spirit of so many people, and I retain my belief in the innate goodness of the vast majority of ordinary and also extraordinary folk, despite evidence to the contrary in other human beings. The welcome kindness of strangers, which I have experienced perhaps more often than I deserve, always restores my faith in human nature.

I am not bound by the practices and teachings of any single religious denomination, and I have often remarked that one of the places where I least find God is in the church annual assemblies, because of the grandstanding and political machinations of many clergy and delegates who attend them. I am sad, however, that the Presbyterianism into which I was baptised by accident of birth has ceased to be a broad and attractive Church and has backed itself into a deeply conservative cul-de-sac. This means that the liberals left in that Church keep their heads down, while other Presbyterian liberals have been voting with their feet and have joined other denominations.

I also take comfort from the earthy advice passed on to me by my beloved Uncle Bill, who lived until his late nineties. He once told me, with his typical broad smile, always to keep positive and to realise that 'every day you are above the ground is a good day!' I read that quote recently from an article in the *Times Saturday Magazine* by Melanie Reid, who is tetraplegic after breaking her neck and back in a riding accident in April 2010. Her courageous, witty and beautifully written weekly column never fails to inspire me.

My personal faith is more instinctive and deeply intuitive than cerebral, and, as I noted earlier, I pay little enough attention to theologians, apart from Paul Tillich. I rely greatly for reassurance on the words of Psalm 23, which I first read so nervously in public as a small boy at a service in Bessbrook Presbyterian Church so long ago. Since then I have come to treasure these words as a great comfort for life and for death.

So, in my long journey so far, I have tried to use my writing to uplift and encourage people where possible, while also reminding readers about the dark sides in so many others. I have found that keeping the faith is not always easy, but I have kept on trying, though some of my questions are still unanswered, and may never be answered on this side of the veil.

Nevertheless, I travel on in hope, while remaining gratefully aware that 'keeping the faith' is a journey and adventure of a lifetime, and perhaps even beyond that. In the final analysis, this is what faith is all about.

Endnotes

1. *Bessbrook: The Model Village 1845–1945* (Bessbrook: Bessbrook Spinning Company Ltd., 2000), p. 23.
2. *Bessbrook: The Model Village*, p. 109.
3. *Bessbrook: The Model Village*, p. 109.
4. Jonathan Bardon, *A History of Ulster* (Belfast: Blackstaff Press, 1992), p. 481.
5. Northern Ireland Parliamentary Debates, 1934, Vol. 16.
6. Alf McCreary, *Healing Touch: An Illustrated History of the Royal College of Physicians* (Dublin: RCPI, 2015), p. 201.
7. Figure supplied by Queen's University Belfast.
8. Andrew Gailey, *Crying in the Wilderness – Jack Sayers, A Liberal Editor in Ulster 1939–69* (Belfast: Institute of Irish Studies at Queen's University Belfast, 1995).
9. Contribution by Bridget Hourican, *Dictionary of Irish Biography* (Cambridge, Cambridge University Press, 2009).
10. Terence O'Neill, *The Autobiography of Terence O'Neill: Prime Minister of Northern Ireland 1963–1969* (London: Rupert Hart-Davis, 1972).
11. O'Neill, *The Autobiography of Terence O'Neill*.
12. Bardon, *History of Ulster*, p. 631.
13. Bardon, *History of Ulster*, p. 634.
14. Gailey, *Crying in the Wilderness*, pp. 103–4.
15. Gailey, *Crying in the Wilderness*, p. 106.
16. Gailey, *Crying in the Wilderness*, p. 138.
17. Bardon, *History of Ulster*, p. 655.
18. O'Neill, *The Autobiography of Terence O'Neill*, pp. 145–9.
19. Gailey, *Crying in the Wilderness*, p. 149.
20. O'Neill, *Crying in the Wilderness*, pp. 140–43.
21. Sidney Elliott and W. D. Flackes, *Northern Ireland: A Political Directory 1968–1999* (Belfast: The Blackstaff Press, 1998), pp. 681–89.
22. Alf McCreary, *Tried By Fire: Finding Hope Out of Suffering* (Basingstoke: Marshall Pickering, 1986), pp. 106–7.
23. McCreary, *Tried By Fire*, p. 112.

24. McCreary, *Tried By Fire*, pp. 52–3.
25. Sophia Hillan King and Seán MacMahon (eds.), *Hope and History: Eyewitness Accounts of Life in Twentieth Century Ulster* (Belfast: Friar's Bush Press, 1996), p. 180.
26. Alf McCreary, *Survivors* (Belfast: Century Books, 1976), p. 144.
27. McCreary, *Survivors*, pp. 139–49.
28. McCreary, *Survivors*, pp. 139–49.
29. Alf McCreary, *Corrymeela: The Search for Peace* (Belfast: Christian Journals Ltd., 1975), p. 33.
30. McCreary, *Corrymeela*, p. 36.
31. McCreary, *Corrymeela*, p. 66.
32. McCreary, *Corrymeela*, p. 57.
33. McCreary, *Tried By Fire*, p. 156.
34. McCreary, *Tried By Fire*, p. 144.
35. Alf McCreary, *In War and Peace – the Story of Corrymeela* (Belfast: The Brehon Press, 2007), p. 251.
36. Gordon Wilson with Alf McCreary, *Marie: A Story from Enniskillen* (London: HarperCollins, 1990), p. 46.
37. Wilson with McCreary, *Marie*, p. 109.
38. Wilson with McCreary, *Marie*, p. 82.
39. Wilson with McCreary, *Marie*, pp. 110–15.
40. Wilson with McCreary, *Marie*, pp. 133–40.
41. Wilson with McCreary, *Marie*, p. 145.
42. Wilson with McCreary, *Marie*, p. 153.
43. Alf McCreary, *Gordon Wilson: An Ordinary Hero* (London: Marshall Pickering, 1990), pp. 15–23.
44. McCreary, *Gordon Wilson*, pp. 41–46.
45. Wilson with McCreary, *Marie*, introduction.
46. McCreary, *Gordon Wilson*, p. 171.
47. McCreary, *Gordon Wilson*, p. 193.
48. Alf McCreary, *A Personal Reflection on Africa Revisited* (London: Tearfund).
49. St Patrick's *Confession*, from the Latin translation by Dr Ludwig Bieler.
50. Derick Bingham, *Patrick – More Than a Legend* (Garvagh: TBF and KL Thompson Trust).
51. Northern Ireland Assembly Debate, 7 February 2000.
52. Alf McCreary, *Belfast Telegraph*, 27 January 2006.
53. John Cooney, *Irish Times*, 17 March 2009.
54. Bardon, *History of Ulster*, pp. 634–35.
55. Elliott and Flackes, *Northern Ireland*, p. 385.

56. William Brown, *Ian Paisley as I Knew Him: Charismatic, Chameleon or Charlatan?* (Belfast: Beyond the Pale Books, 2022), xi.

57. *Belfast Newsletter*, 26 October 2023.

58. G. K. Chesterton, *What's Wrong with the World* (London: Cassell, 1910).

59. C. S. Lewis, *Mere Christianity* (London: Geoffrey Bles, 1952).

Acknowledgements

I would like to thank a number of people, including the staff of Messenger Publications, in particular the Director Cecilia West who first saw its potential and supported me throughout the various stages of the research and writing. I would also like to thank Messenger's Production and Sales Coordinator Ellen Murray, Art Director Brendan McCarthy, Senior Editor Kate Kiernan, Editor Fiona Biggs, and Communications and Marketing Executive Carolanne Henry for their help with the editing, design, production and launch of *Keeping the Faith*.

I would also like to thank the Right Reverend the Lord Eames OM who read the manuscript and provided a perceptive foreword in which he captured the essence of the book. Robin and I have worked closely together for many years on other projects, and I am delighted professionally and also personally that he agreed to become associated with this memoir.

I extend my thanks to the publishers and authors of the various books and other publications from which I have quoted and which are mentioned in the endnotes, as well as those whose quotations I have included from newspapers and other media sources, and also the help from the staff members of the Linen Hall Library in Belfast.

Finally, I would also like to thank my wife Hilary who has been such a strong supporter during the research and writing of this book and also throughout the research and writing of so many other books and articles during our long and closely-shared journey of life.

Alf McCreary